SAINT JOHN HENRY
NEWMAN

SAINT JOHN HENRY

NEWMAN

His Life and Works

*All books are published
thanks to the generosity of the supporters
of the Catholic Truth Society*

Biographical material taken from: *John Henry Newman, Apostle to the Doubtful* by Meriol Trevor, revised and expanded by Léonie Caldecott (first published 2001 by The Incorporated Catholic Truth Society, 40-46 Harleyford Road, London SE11 5AY. Copyright © 2001 CTS); apart from the final section, on Newman's beatification and canonisation, which is from *Newman: his Life & Legacy* by Fr Ian Ker (first published 2010 by CTS; revised edition 2019. Copyright © 2010, 2019 CTS). Writings taken from: *The Mind of Cardinal Newman* (ed. Charles Dessain) (first published 1974 by CTS, reprinted 1994, 2010; Copyright © 1974, 1994, 2010 CTS) and *Daily Christian Living with John Henry Newman* (first published 2009; Copyright © CTS 2009). Sermons: II & III originally published (collected) in *Discourses Addressed to Mixed Congregations* (1849), individually reprinted CTS 1892, 1939, 1952; individually in *Sermons Preached on Various Occasions* (1874), reprinted CTS n.d. (by 1912).

Images: Front cover, *Cardinal John Henry Newman*, 1888 © Chronicle/Alamy Stock Photo. Back cover, three images of John Henry Newman © 2019, National Institute for Newman Studies, All rights reserved. Inside colour section © Mazur/catholicchurch.org.uk apart from: Portrait of *John Henry Newman* by William Charles Ross © GL Archive/Alamy Stock Photo. Oriel College, Oxford © David Ionut/Shutterstock.com. University Church of St Mary the Virgin, Oxford © Kevin Standage/Shutterstock.com. Desk in Newman's personal library © Fr James Bradley. Chasubles worn by Newman © Fr James Bradley. Reliquary, Birmingham Oratory © Fr Lawrence Lew, OP.

ISBN 978 1 78469 621 4

Contents

Foreword

A few weeks before he died, St John Henry Newman replied to an address from the newly established Catholic Truth Society, which was then meeting in Birmingham. In it he congratulated the Society on their aim of producing Catholic literature and teaching in a form, and at a price, which made it accessible to the widest possible audience. It is fitting, therefore, that his canonisation is being celebrated by the publication of this anthology of his writing, and I warmly commend it to those who want to know why it is that Newman has been raised to the altars of the Church.

It is probably impossible to say what St John Henry Newman's most important contribution to the life of the Church is. As this anthology makes clear, many different answers are possible. For some he is the poet of *The Dream of Gerontius*; for others, he is the philosopher of *The Grammar of Assent*; for others, too, he is the theologian of *An Essay on the Development of Christian Doctrine*; and finally, he is the genius who combined poetry, philosophy and theology in what is, arguably, his most famous work, the *Apologia pro Vita Sua*. But if one had to identify the one thing that makes him such an important saint for our times, one might say that it was his intelligent confrontation with modernity. Writing of St Philip Neri, Newman said:

> he perceived that the mischief [i.e. of modernity] was to be met, not with argument, not with science, not with protests and warnings, not by the recluse or the preacher, but by means of the great counter-fascination of purity and truth.

Purity and truth might be said to be the two things that Newman sought all his life. For him, purity was something more than continence; it was the single-mindedness with which he followed the "kindly light" which led him, one step at a time, from what the historian Edward Gibbon described as "the port and prejudice of Oxford" to the converted gin palace in Alcester Street, Birmingham, where he set up the Oratory of St Philip Neri in England. Truth for Newman was something far greater than a philosopher's quibble; it was the great goal of all human striving and the final destination towards which all men and women are journeying, whether they know it or not. Newman famously described the *transitus* from this life to the life of eternity as a journey *ex umbris et imaginibus in veritatem* — from shadows and images into truth. As an Oxford don, Newman was a skilled Latinist, and it is therefore no accident that he should have chosen to put the word *veritatem* in the accusative case, for in Latin, when the word *in* takes the accusative it means "into". For Newman, truth was something dynamic, something living. Ultimately, it was God, and it is his single-minded pursuit of God that surely gives the key to his sanctity.

However, Newman also realised that the pursuit of purity and truth comes at a cost, since it is a pursuit which is made in a culture which values neither. One of his most famous sermons – which is reproduced in this anthology – is *The Second Spring*. After celebrating in lyrical language the fact that,

> Westminster and Nottingham, Beverley and Hexham, Northampton and Shrewsbury, if the world lasts, shall be names as musical to the ear, as stirring to the heart, as the glories we have lost

and that,

> saints shall rise out of them, if God so will, and doctors once again shall give the law to Israel, and preachers call to penance and to justice, as at the beginning.

Newman throws a metaphorical bucket of cold water over his audience by reminding them that,

> not saints alone, not doctors only, not preachers only, shall be ours – but martyrs, too, shall reconsecrate the soil to God...[and that]...if the truth is to be spread to any wide extent among this people, how can we dream, how can we hope, that trial and trouble shall not accompany its going forth?

There must have been many who thought that he was exaggerating at this point. The culture of Victorian liberalism which Newman confronted assumed that

Catholicism was ridiculous and it could be proved to be so by the certainties of the religion of science. There could be no question, in the England of Edward Smith Stanley, the 14th Earl of Derby who was the Prime Minister at the time Newman preached his sermon, of anyone going to prison, or losing his life, for preaching the Catholic faith. History, however, has proved Newman's analysis to be prophetic. This anthology is being published in a culture which is characterised by an aggressive secular liberalism which refuses to admit that there is such a thing as absolute truth and which is parting company to an ever greater extent with the Christian culture from which it is, nevertheless, derived. As the great Catholic historian Christopher Dawson put it,

> a confederacy of evil, marshalling its hosts from all parts of the world, organising itself, taking its measures, is enclosing the Church of Christ as in a net.

The vision which Newman foresaw perhaps reaches its consummation in the gulags and the killing fields of the twentieth century, and it is more than coincidental that Sophie Scholl, one of the founders of the White Rose resistance movement in Nazi Germany, found in Newman's writings the intellectual and spiritual resources to make sense of the brutal and demonic world around her.

The brutality and evil which cost Sophie Scholl her life may be less obvious in the Britain of Boris Johnson or the America of Donald Trump. However, there is much in modern Western culture that is equally opposed to that transcendent vision of human life and destiny which inspired St John Henry Newman and which runs like a *leitmotif* through everything that he did and said. It is difficult to know whether Newman would have laughed or wept at the news that a bishop of the Established Church had written a prayer for use on the occasion of an abortion, but he would certainly have seen in the inhumane holocaust of abortion and euthanasia a fundamental denial of the dignity of the human person.

St John Henry Newman saw more than that. He saw all of human life through the lens of eternity. At the end of his sermon *God's Will the End of Life*, which concludes this anthology he reminds his hearers that,

the world passes; it is but a pageant and a scene; the lofty palace crumbles, the busy city is mute, the ships of Tarshish have sped away. On heart and flesh death is coming; the veil is breaking. Departing soul, how hast thou used thy talents, thy opportunities, the light poured around thee, the warnings given thee, the grace inspired into thee? O my Lord and Saviour, support me in that hour in the strong arms of thy Sacraments, and by the fresh fragrance of thy consolations. Let the absolving words be said over me, and the holy oil sign and seal me, and thy own Body be my food, and thy Blood my sprinkling; and let my sweet Mother Mary breathe on me, and my angel whisper peace to me, and my glorious saints, and my own dear father, Philip, smile on me; that in them all, and through them all, I may receive the gift of perseverance, and die, as I desire to live, in thy faith, in thy Church, in thy service, and in thy love.

This is a vision of hope, a vision inspired by the belief that since life in this world is a preparation for the life to come, the only final tragedy is to leave it unprepared. St John Henry Newman shows us in this anthology how we make those preparations and how we may, like him, journey from shadows and images *into* the truth.

Fr Ignatius Harrison
The Oratory
Birmingham

Preface

As John Henry Newman is recognised by the Church as a saint — that is, as someone whose intercession for us is powerful and whose witness to Christ is strong — it may be helpful to provide a brief introduction to his life and writings for those who do not know him.

The following text is an abridgement of a number of short booklets from the CTS archives giving both an account of Newman's life and numerous thematically arranged short extracts from his (very considerable) written works, so as to give some notion of the range and value of his thought.

We have also included three sermons as an example of how Newman's writing works over a larger compass.

Readers can of course explore Newman's writings further through the various good modern editions of them. There are also several longer biographies that give a fuller account of his life and times, and numerous studies examining his thought under different aspects.

The pastoral work that formed so great a part of Newman's life is carried on to this day by the various English houses of the Oratorian Fathers.

PART I

A BRIEF LIFE OF
JOHN HENRY NEWMAN

The Early Years

On the night of 8th October 1845, in the midst of
a heavy rainstorm, an Italian Passionist priest called
Dominic Barberi arrived at Littlemore, a small village
just outside Oxford. Father Dominic had been riding
on the top of the coach and was soaked to the skin.
His destination was some converted stables, where the
famous Anglican preacher John Henry Newman and
some of his friends were living whilst they attempted
to discern the will of God for their lives. As the
missionary priest was attempting to dry his worn and
shabby clothes in front of the fire, Newman came into
the room and cast himself at his feet. He asked to be
received into "the one Fold of the Redeemer", and
then began to make his general confession.

That confession continued the following day, as
did those of two of Newman's companions, and in
the evening they all made the profession of faith and
received conditional baptism. On 10th October, the
very table on which Newman had spent the previous
few years writing *On the Development of Christian
Doctrine* was used to celebrate Mass during which
Newman received his first Holy Communion.

Newman was then obliged to leave his peaceful haven at Littlemore in order to place himself at the service of the Church. He was at the midpoint of his life, no longer a young man, with a wealth of learning and experience behind him, and yet he submitted himself completely to a new life, leaving behind uncomprehending and often unsympathetic friends and family. After years of holding a respected position as Fellow of Oriel College Oxford and the Vicar of the University Church, not to mention his central role in the Anglican "Oxford Movement", he was now to be instructed and prepared for the priesthood in Rome alongside much younger and less qualified men. Newman did this, peaceful in the knowledge that after years of painstaking deliberation, he had made the right choice. He had said that he wanted to be sure to act from reason, not from feeling alone.

The weather that evening in October 1845 reflected to some extent Newman's own life. He was beset by storms and controversies, both as an Anglican and as a Catholic. A man of powerful intellect, he nonetheless submitted his mind to that of the Church, even in the midst of misunderstandings and intense debate. Newman was possessed by the love of God to such a degree that he gave his whole life over to his service, a devotion which showed as much in his pastoral work among ordinary people, as in his thought and writing.

A man of the nineteenth century

Born on 21st February 1801, John Henry Newman lived through the turbulent nineteenth century, when

Europe was struggling with wars and revolutions, political and intellectual.

John Henry Newman saw the Christian Church as an historical fact, its ideas and practice in continual but consistent development. This historical way of looking at the Church's ideas was quite new when Newman wrote his *An Essay on the Development of Christian Doctrine* in 1845. From this historical base Newman was able to build a defence of the truth of Christian tradition in answer to the scientific scepticism that was spreading among educated people.

Newman realised that rationalising methods of inquiry would attack the credibility of the Bible. He perceived that it was the Church which mediated the revelation in Christ. It was in studying the early Fathers of the Church that Newman realised how theological ideas had developed over the centuries, like a tree growing from a seed. That seed was Christ, the Word of God.

Search for the truth

His first conversion, to which he gave a duration of five months (prompting some Evangelicals in later years to assure him he had never been converted at all) he called in the *Apologia* "a great change of thought" and indeed the books lent him by Mr Mayers, a young Evangelical master at his school, first started Newman thinking about the Christian religion. *The Force of Truth* by Thomas Scott, a Unitarian who had thought his way to belief in the Trinity of God and the Incarnation of the Son, or Word, in the man Jesus of Nazareth, not only implanted in Newman's mind the doctrine itself but presented religious truth as a quest and the understanding of it as a personal development. Scott's sayings, "Holiness before peace" and "Growth the only evidence of life," became proverbs for the young Newman. From the start Christianity was for him not merely a system to be accepted, but a way of life.

Milner's *Church History* had an equally profound effect, for there Newman first discovered the Fathers of the Church, the great Christian thinkers of the early centuries. He was shown the way into a world where the supreme mysteries were neither devitalised into an abstract system, nor subjected to the degenerative process of uncontrolled feeling. Moreover, he was introduced to the Church as it was before the period of medieval Christendom, out of which had burst the Protestant revolution. So, in 1816, at the age of fifteen, Newman started on the path that was to make him an agent of reform in the Church of England and later to draw him, slowly and painfully, into the Catholic Church in communion with the see of St Peter.

Education and early years in the Anglican Church

John Henry was the eldest of six children and the leader in their games, writing plays for them to act. Their father was a banker, one of the rising middle class, and their mother, Jemima Fourdrinier, was the daughter of a papermaker of Huguenot descent.

After a happy childhood Newman was sent to a private school at Ealing, where he did so well that he was accepted at Trinity College Oxford when he was only sixteen. At first he over-worked and did badly in his final examinations, but was able to stay on at the university to prepare for ordination because he had earlier won a college scholarship. In 1822, when he was just twenty-one, he was elected a Fellow of Oriel College, then the centre of intellectual excellence. This was the start of an academic career and a regular income, much needed. His father had never recovered his position after his bankruptcy and died in 1824, leaving Newman responsible for finding a home for his mother and sisters, and for his brother Frank's education. Besides coaching Frank, he made some money by taking other pupils.

That year Newman had been ordained deacon and took on an arduous curacy at St Clement's, on the edge of Oxford. He was ordained a priest in the Church of England at Whitsun, 29th May 1825. "I was dedicating myself forever, consecrating myself to the service of Almighty God," he wrote many years later.

When in 1828 he was made Vicar of the University Church of St Mary the Virgin, he gained a position of considerable influence in Oxford. The Tractarian Movement, which got under way in 1833, was originally a protest against state interference in church affairs. It was Newman who wrote the first *Tracts for the Times* on this subject, short and to the point.

Italy and the Oxford Movement

In 1833, Newman and a friend, Hurrell Froude, travelled to Italy on vacation. He had the chance to observe a number of Catholic devotions, and his impression of the Roman Catholic Church as corrupt and spiritually decayed began to change, even though the religious practices of the Italians felt culturally alien. The experience of another illness, serious enough to be life-threatening, whilst staying alone in Sicily, marked a watershed for Newman. It is here that he wrote his famous poem, "Lead Kindly Light", and pledged himself to undertake the work of renewing and purifying the Church of England, no matter what the cost. Immediately on his return, Keble preached his famous sermon "On National Apostasy" and so the Oxford Movement was launched.

The *Tracts* of the Movement were delivered by keen adherents to vicarages around the country. Newman rode out on horseback to deliver some himself. The Movement caused great excitement in the 1830s, especially among the young, stirring them up to consider the nature of the Church and its position vis-à-vis the State, with which it had been inextricably entwined ever since King Henry VIII had declared himself head of the Church in England. Newman had realised that the Church had always conceived itself to be an autonomous community – communion – and catholic, that is, universal, supra-national, with the bishops as guardians of the Apostolic faith.

Newman's influence grew not only from the *Tracts* (unsigned), but from his sermons, which because he published them in a series of books reached a nationwide audience. Readers, expecting controversial Catholic views, were faced instead with a psychologically penetrating preaching of Christ the Lord, the Christ of the Gospels, and the challenge he presents to all to change their lives in following him.

From 1833 till 1841 Newman was the chief instigator of the Oxford Movement, which aroused strong opposition from the majority of establishment men. For many, *Tract 90* was the last straw. Newman argued that the Thirty-Nine Articles, which had to be signed by all ministers of the Church of England and all members of the university, were not so much a protest against the Catholic faith, as against medieval errors and corruptions. They could therefore be taken in a Catholic sense. This was essential to the case that the Church of England was part of the Catholic Church. But it provoked an uproar in London and in Oxford, where Newman acknowledged his authorship in answer to a censure from the university authorities. London papers proclaimed that popery was unmasked at Oxford. This was the beginning of the legend of Newman as a dissimulating and secret papist.

The Littlemore years

It was also the beginning of Newman's retreat to Littlemore, an outlying part of St Mary's parish, where he had built a small church in 1836 and started a school for the poor children of the village. Here we see Newman's pastoral side coming to the fore. He personally taught the children their catechism, and how to sing the psalms. He kept a rigorous Lent each year, with severe fasting, though he walked into Oxford most days to perform his duties there. He converted some stable buildings into a simple residence, where he was soon joined by various young men who were also beginning to feel that there was no place for them in a Church of England which maintained its Protestantism so vociferously.

During the years at Littlemore, Newman, who had stopped the *Tracts* at his bishop's request, had to endure condemnation from almost all the bishops, thus demonstrating to him that they repudiated the role of guardians of the Catholic and Apostolic faith, except as it had been reformed in the sixteenth century. Newman gave up St Mary's in 1843, and lived at Littlemore as a layman, the services being said there by his curate and friend, William John Copeland. Newman himself used the Roman Breviary, the volumes that had belonged to his friend Hurrell Froude, who died in 1836.

The process of moving from the Church of England to the Catholic Church was painful for Newman. Conscience seemed to be prising him out of his life's work and away from his oldest friends towards a Church which in England had long been suppressed under penal laws, lifted only in 1829, and consequently was little known, few in numbers and with few educational opportunities.

The development of Christian doctrine

In writing *An Essay on the Development of Christian Doctrine*, Newman concluded that although there had been some corruptions in practice, and devotional exaggerations, the changes in doctrine had been the result of collective meditation on the original revelation by God in Christ, and that the Church in all ages had been guided into all truth by the Holy Spirit, as Christ had promised. The characteristics of authentic doctrinal development are analogous to those of a well-functioning body. The Church is such a body: the Body of Christ on earth.

Newman was received into the Catholic Church on 9th October 1845. It is perhaps significant that the man who received him was a priest whose principal mission was to the poor in the industrial Midlands. It was in that context that Blessed Dominic Barberi's most famous convert would serve the Roman Catholic Church for the remaining forty-five years of his life.

The Later Years

Ordination and the Oratory

One of the worst trials of Newman's last year at
Littlemore had been the many letters he had received
as the result of a report in the papers that he had
already gone over to Rome, many berating him, but
others, more painful, from anguished Tractarians who
felt he was deserting them. His actual conversion
was followed by an exodus from the Church of
England of professional men, clergy, lawyers, doctors,
schoolmasters and their families, which naturally
enraged the public, the newspapers, Parliament and
Protestants of all parties. Newman himself was given
a temporary home, with his younger disciples, at
Old Oscott College, outside Birmingham, which
he rechristened Maryvale (he also took Maria as his
confirmation name). But he was soon sent to Rome,
with Ambrose St John, to study for the priesthood.
There, at the College of Propaganda Fide, he was
ordained a Catholic priest, and said his first Mass on
the feast of Corpus Christi 1847.

After much prayer and discussion with his band of young ex-Oxford men, Newman decided to join the Congregation of the Oratory, a religious institute which had grown up around the charismatic St Philip Neri, a Florentine who spent nearly all his long life in turbulent sixteenth century Rome.

When his devoted disciples determined to form a community St Philip insisted that they should not take monastic vows, but each keep their own property so as to be free to leave if he wished. The priests were to live together, following a Rule of life, forming in towns a centre for lay people to gather and deepen their understanding of the faith. This seemed to Newman the community best suited to his university converts and also for the expanding industrial towns of England, which he regarded as the future seats of influence. For this reason he was content to be sent to Birmingham, where Nicholas Wiseman, the patron of the converts, was Bishop of the Midland District, with his seat at Pugin's redbrick Gothic College of (new) Oscott.

Newman had been authorised to adapt the sixteenth century Oratorian Rule for nineteenth century England, and in February 1848 he formally set up the Oratory at Maryvale. The first year was full of the human problems of forming into a community the various individuals who wanted to stay with Newman. At the beginning of 1849 he moved into Birmingham, where he had bought the lease of an old gin distillery in the backstreets of Deritend, converting the large room once filled with vats into a chapel. Here, almost at once, rather to Newman's surprise, poor factory children came crowding in every evening, "like herrings in season", as he said. They worked so late in the presswork factories that he could not start a school for them, but he formed a choir for boys and girls, and the young Fathers instructed them in the faith. For the next few years Newman was living here, working hard and so short of money that he could not even afford a pair of new shoes.

Reaction and counter-reaction

The restoration in 1850 of the Catholic hierarchy (with territorial dioceses instead of mission districts) caused the biggest anti-papal uproar since the Gordon Riots of 1780, with hostile articles in *The Times*, cartoons in *Punch* (cadaverous Newman appearing almost as often as rotund Wiseman), angry public meetings of respectable people up and down the country, mob attacks on convents, pelting of suspected priests with mud and stones. Bonfires were lit, with effigies of the Pope and Wiseman burning on top.

Disturbances continued into 1851 and in the summer Newman gave a series of lectures at the Birmingham Corn Exchange on *The Present Position of Catholics in England*, intended to calm 'No-Popery' passions. He demonstrated the absurdity of the anti-Catholic legends by inventing parodies – for instance, ignorant foreigners misinterpreting legal phrases such as "the King can do no wrong" as meaning that the British believed their monarch impeccable and sinless. The audience laughed and went away enlightened.

The Achilli affair

In the course of the lectures Newman made a written attack on an ex-priest, the notorious Italian Giacomo Achilli, who was touring the country, backed by the Protestant Alliance, posing as a victim of the Inquisition for conscience sake, with lurid tales of torture and clerical vice. Wiseman had exposed Achilli's real character in the *Dublin Review*, saying that he had been brought to court in Rome for the serial seduction of young women, expelled from the Dominican order and sentenced to detention in a monastery – from which he had escaped. Few people other than Catholics read the *Dublin Review*, but everybody read Newman, and the Protestant Alliance persuaded Achilli to bring a libel case against the Apostate Newman, as the press called him.

Newman had relied on Wiseman's papers to justify him, but as the cardinal had mislaid them, he was forced to get direct evidence from abroad, including several of women from Italy, who were chaperoned by Maria Giberne, a family friend who had followed Newman into the Church. When the trial at last began, Achilli brazenly denied all the charges. The jury held that Newman had proved none of them, except that Achilli had been deprived of his lectureship. Newman's lawyers asked for a new trial, but it was refused, and on 31st January 1853 Newman was sentenced to a £100 fine and jail until it was paid. He had been prepared for prison, with his portmanteau packed, but his friends paid up on the spot. Newman received from the judge a severe lecture on his moral deterioration since his conversion to Rome.

Although the Achilli Trial reduced Newman's reputation among Protestants, it raised it among Catholics, who regarded him as their champion. They subscribed to a fund for his expenses and cheered him loudly as he left the court. But it had been a gruelling experience, especially trying to Newman in the suspense and uncertainty which were still hanging over him when he was asked to preach the sermon at the first Synod of the restored hierarchy in 1852. He called it *The Second Spring* – the Catholic Church rising again in England after a winter three hundred years long.

Dublin and The Idea of a University

The same year, he went over to Ireland to deliver his lectures on *The Idea of a University*, at the Rotunda in Dublin, where he had been invited by Archbishop Cullen to found a Catholic university. Newman was not inaugurated as Rector until 1854, though he had taken a house and put things in motion before that. Newman's struggles to found the Catholic university on the right lines were prolonged and exhausting, hampered as he was by Cullen's suspicions of his aims at a liberal education for laymen. It was Cullen who prevented Newman's being made a (titular) bishop, which Wiseman thought he had secured for him, spreading the news around, which became very embarrassing when nothing happened. Newman would have accepted it solely because it would have given him a seat on the university commission. Later he was glad of the omission, since it left him freer to pursue his own work.

Newman made many lay friends in Ireland, but this only increased the clerical mistrust. Yet he succeeded in setting up faculties, appointing well-qualified lecturers and starting examinations. He also presided over a group of students from various countries who lived in his own house. (He shocked Cullen by allowing them a billiard table). He was also able to build a university church out of the remainder of the fund raised for his defence in the Achilli Trial.

Blessings in Rome

In Rome, during a private audience with the Pope, Pius IX, Newman told him of his community's work at the prison, the workhouse, the orphanage and poor schools. The Holy Father was very pleased, saying that this was an age for active works. Besides his blessing the Pope gave them a Paschal Candle and his own picture of St Philip.

A new translation of the Bible

Wiseman asked Newman to supervise the production of a new English translation of the Bible. Newman had consulted seminary professors who were enthusiastic, and urged him to abandon the chapter and verse arrangement in favour of paragraphing. He appointed his team, among them Fr Ambrose St John, who had studied Hebrew under Pusey, and Fr Edward Caswall, the Latinist translator of many ancient hymns still sung today. But now, when he wrote asking if he could hold the copyright for a year or so, to finance the work, he got no reply. It was Wiseman's way of dropping the whole project. Catholics in England had to wait another hundred years for a new translation.

The Rambler *and the role of the laity*

Soon afterwards there arose in Rome some suspicions concerning Fr Newman's orthodoxy, or lack of it. This came about through his connection with the *Rambler*, a bimonthly magazine which had been started by a convert clergyman, John Moore Capes, whom Newman had advised. In 1858 *The Rambler* was acquired by the young Sir John Acton, scion of an old Catholic family.

Newman saw the need for a high quality literary magazine with a Catholic, but not a narrow, outlook and continued to advise. Unfortunately, one of the lively-minded staff of *The Rambler* could not resist quoting historical scandals and making his points in a polemical way – "discharging peashooters at cardinals who happened to pass by the window" as Newman remarked to Acton. The newly restored Catholic hierarchy in England were not amused by such peashooters and threatened censure, which would have deprived the magazine of most of its readers. Newman was asked to mediate but the bishops stipulated that the proprietors must resign the editorship. They said they would only do so if they could hand the paper over to Newman. Eventually he accepted, intending to delete any remarks that could be "offensive to pious ears" and to introduce a correspondence section so that differing views could be aired without editorial responsibility.

It was Newman himself who caused further offence to episcopal ears, through a comment on education. Public pronouncements had been made about education without any consultation with the laity, the persons most concerned. Newman observed that if the faithful had been consulted about the recent definition of the Immaculate Conception of the Blessed Virgin Mary, they should surely be so consulted in matters of education. When exception was taken to this, he wrote an article entitled *On Consulting the Faithful in Matter of Doctrine*. He used the word "consult" in the sense of "consulting a barometer" – finding out the belief of the laity, not of giving them voting power, so to speak, in the decisions of the magisterium. He also pointed out that in the early centuries it was often the laity who kept orthodox faith alive, even when various bishops opposed it, as in the Arian crisis.

This article, pointing out the role of the faithful laity in the Church, was related to Rome by Bishop Brown of Newport, as part of an attack on the recent converts, whose habits of free speech made them suspect to the old Catholic clergy. Newman did not hear of this until early in the new year of 1860, when his own bishop, Ullathorne, told him of it. He immediately wrote to Wiseman, asking to be sent the passages complained of, so that he could endeavour to explain them, since he had certainly not said that the Church could fail in matters of doctrine. Wiseman was in Rome, and did nothing about it. Later Ullathorne, when in Rome himself, was given to understand that something was being done, and so Newman assumed that it had been decided not to pursue it. But in fact Cardinal Barnabò at Propaganda was left thinking that Newman had failed to answer charges which he knew had been made against him. The suspicion of unorthodoxy continued to hang over Newman in Rome for another seven years.

The *Rambler* episode came in 1859 when Newman was in the midst of starting a school, persuaded by his lay convert friends who did not want to send their sons to seminaries. By this time, Newman had resigned from the Catholic university, partly because he could not get the backing he needed – a Vice Rector chosen by himself and a finance committee of laymen. In spite of all the difficulties with Cardinal Cullen (who was reporting adversely to Rome on his activities) Newman had set things going and founded a Medical School which was to flourish and endure. He also started evening classes for the "mechanics", working men, years before Oxford attempted any such thing.

Daily duties

In 1857 Newman retired from Ireland. He felt his presence was needed in England. He foresaw the great trial of faith that was coming with the advance of scientific scepticism, which he felt he might help to counter, by using reason to demonstrate the credibility of Christianity. This was for Newman a personal motif, carried through from his Anglican to his Catholic days, from his sermons on Reason and Faith, and the *Essay on Development*, to the *Grammar of Assent*.

The most urgent need for him was in Birmingham, if his conception of the Oratory was to bear fruit.

Newman was always practical; he distrusted much that was spoken of as 'spirituality' and noticed that spiritual enthusiasts often shunned hard pastoral work among the poor. He advised seekers after perfection to do the duties of the day, however humdrum, as perfectly as possible. He followed his own advice, taking up all his old duties as a priest on his return from Ireland. Many people, then and afterwards, did not realise what a devoted pastoral ministry Newman was carrying out in the industrial city of Birmingham. But his parishioners, to the third and fourth generation, knew how to value it, and loved him for it.

The Oratory School

The Oratory School opened in 1859 in buildings adjacent to the church and house, and was a success, but for Newman, who was officially in charge of it, success itself proved at first a source of great anxiety. This was because the headmaster, Fr Nicholas Darnell, a brilliant and energetic man, was ambitious to rival the great public schools of the day and secretly planned with rich lay friends to move it out of its unfashionable Birmingham surroundings altogether. However, this would have been against the Rule, as it would have meant taking Fathers to work outside their community. Fr Darnell came into conflict with the school matron, Mrs Wootten, the widow of Newman's Oxford doctor, who got to hear of these plans and knew they would not meet with Newman's approval. Darnell called her a spy, and in 1861 at Christmas time, this developed into an open row. Darnell threatened that either she must go, or he would go. Faced with Darnell's ultimatum, Newman refused to sack Mrs Wootten, whose care of the younger boys he considered very important, and he also disapproved of Darnell's reliance on flogging. Whereupon Darnell and the entire lay staff resigned, just before the beginning of term in January 1862.

Newman rose to the challenge and accepted the staff resignations, though he tried to keep Fr Darnell from leaving the Oratory. He appointed Fr Ambrose St John as headmaster and managed to secure several well-qualified laymen, including Tom Arnold, the convert son of Dr Arnold of Rugby (whom he had already employed in Dublin) to fill the vacancies. He took some classes himself and soon began producing the Latin plays he had acted in long ago at Ealing School – and he did it with great verve, the boys remembered. Darnell, who was in a highly overwrought state, did leave the Oratory. But he and his friends talked freely in London, gossiping that Newman favoured the opinions of an old woman over the schoolmasters'. It was even said that the boys were not given proper religious instruction. This was nonsense, and Newman often gave it himself. In later years Darnell wrote to Newman with a heartfelt apology for what he had done.

The dark night

Worn down by more than ten years' hard work for the Church, most of which seemed not to have come to fruition, and to have earned him suspicion and denigration, Newman was now suffering from a feeling of rejection similar to the one he had endured after

Tract 90. Trying to understand what had happened to him since 1845, Newman wrote down some of his thoughts in an exercise book, first in December 1859 and January 1860, and then again in January 1863: "What am I living for? What am I doing for any religious end?" Typically, he approached the painful present by thinking over his past life. "O how forlorn and dreary has been my course since I have been a Catholic! Here has been the contrast – as a Protestant I felt my religion dreary, but not my life – but, as a Catholic, my life dreary, not my religion."

In his depleted Oratory in Birmingham, he carried on with his immediate duties as a priest, often holding the fort while the other Fathers took holidays, acting as sacristan, dusting the books in the library and making notes on "Certitude" which were to become the *Essay in Aid of a Grammar of Assent.* His mind was certainly as acute as ever. He was persuaded to take some holidays himself, paid for by the other Fathers when they discovered that he himself could not afford it. From Deal and other places Newman wrote some amusing letters home, describing the seaside lodgings, the meals, and the disappointment of getting the latest novel from the local library and finding it "more and more [unpleasant] like medicine".

Kingsley and the Apologia

Newman found himself attacked in a review by the popular novelist, Charles Kingsley, who caricatured him as the typical representative of a corrupt and lying Roman Catholic clergy.

Truth for its own sake has never been a virtue with the Roman clergy. Father Newman informs us that it need not, and on the whole ought not to be; that cunning is the weapon which heaven has given to the saints wherewith to withstand the brute male force of the wicked world which marries and is given in marriage. Whether his notion is doctrinally correct or no, at least it is historically so.

Newman did not recognise the "C.K." signature as that of Charles Kingsley, then at the height of his literary reputation, a chaplain to the Queen and tutor to the Prince of Wales. He thought it must be "a young scribe who is making a cheap reputation by smart hits at safe objects," as he said to the publisher, Alexander Macmillan, when writing to demand an apology. But the paragraph which Kingsley grudgingly composed was almost more insulting than the original one, accepting that Newman had not meant what he had said in an Oxford sermon on Wisdom and Innocence. Newman countered with an amusing dialogue printed as a short pamphlet, which caught the attention of journalists and was reprinted in numerous periodicals. "Mean it! I maintain I never said it, whether as a Protestant or a Catholic," he insisted. Enraged by this squib's success, Kingsley launched into a long and furious diatribe – *What then does Dr Newman mean?* in which all his prejudices against priests, celibacy, confessionals, moral equivocations and ecclesiastical power politics came pouring out.

Newman received this pamphlet on Palm Sunday, at the Birmingham Oratory, just after he had sung the principal Mass. At first he almost despaired of meeting effectively "such a heap of misrepresentation and such a vehemence of animosity." But then he decided that what gave Kingsley's accusations their force was his belief that he was attacking a liar – not specific dissimulations so much as a man who was fundamentally untrustworthy and had found his right place in a religious system which inevitably issued in moral corruption. The best way of answering him, Newman thought, was "to give the true key to my whole life; I must show what I am that it may be seen what I am not, and that the phantom may be extinguished which gibbers instead of me ... I will draw out the history of my mind ..." In the process, he would be able to defend the Church and his fellow priests as well as himself.

The *Apologia pro Vita Sua* – the defence of his life – had to be written at speed, the parts published (by Longman) as he wrote them, weekly, through April and May and into June 1863. He worked all day, once for twenty-two hours with the printer's man waiting at the door, and yet he was determined to quote contemporary letters and check facts with some old Anglican friends who had recently made contact with him after a silence of nearly twenty years. Besides this, he wrote so fairly and charitably of Anglican enemies who had snubbed and thwarted him in days gone by, that several wrote to thank him. His tributes to all those he had learned from caused some reviewers, ironically, to wonder why he had been credited with any ideas of his own.

In the *Apologia* Newman not only vindicated his own reputation for honesty and the pursuit of truth at all costs, but in the last part he set forth the case for a divine revelation in the face of the great mysteries of human existence. This approach appealed to a new generation, including such diverse spirits as Gerard Manley Hopkins (who was received into the Church by Newman) and Thomas Hardy. With his *Apologia*, because it was a personal history, not controversial, Newman advanced the process of understanding between English Protestants and Catholics immeasurably.

The Dream of Gerontius

Shortly after the *Apologia*, another, very different, work also won new respect for its author. This was the long poem (later set to music by Elgar) *The Dream of Gerontius*, which was published in 1865. It encapsulates Newman's vision of the journey made by the soul after death. It explains the Catholic doctrine of purgatory by demonstrating even a righteous soul's response to the proximity of God. Faced with the contrast between his perfection and its own lack, the soul requests its Guardian Angel to take it to purgatory so that it may purify and prepare itself adequately for the Beatific Vision.

Gladstone, a devout Anglican, wrote to Newman, "I own that it seems to me the most remarkable production in its own very high walk since the unapproachable *Paradiso* of Dante." Even Charles Kingsley, writing to a friend in 1868, admitted, "I read with awe and admiration."

Further controversies and the struggle for certitude

This revival of Newman's personal influence alarmed men like Manning, who became Archbishop of Westminster in 1865, when Wiseman died. Manning already regarded Newman as not sufficiently Roman a Catholic, and now he thought him positively dangerous, encouraging the laity in their worldly and national ambitions, and promoting "the school of literary vanities." In particular he was determined that Newman should never go to Oxford again, since his presence would lure young Catholics to the university where they would assuredly lose their faith. He therefore secured and maintained a veto from Rome on Catholics going there, just when university reform measures had at last allowed them entrance.

Bishop Ullathorne twice tried to get Newman to Oxford, to take on the mission there, and later to build a church and start an Oratory, but each time Manning, through his allies in Rome, managed to prevent it. When a cardinal was sent to inquire into the educational situation, he was kept away from Newman, and the Oratory School was never put on the list with other schools to be visited. As to returning to Oxford himself, Newman was in two minds, but he did think an Oratory would be the best way of assisting young Catholics to grow in their faith while receiving an education they could not then receive anywhere else. Newman was always thinking of how to meet the world on its own ground, and convert it.

In 1870, *An Essay in Aid of a Grammar of Assent* was published. It sets out to demonstrate the philosophical underpinnings of religious belief. Employing a style of reasoning which goes beyond classical scholastic philosophy, the essay shows how it can be right to believe what one cannot understand or prove, by distinguishing the 'notional' apprehension of an abstraction, from the 'real' apprehension of a thing. The believer gives real assent to the existence of God and the authority of the Church, because the various evidences for these converge not on an abstraction, but on a concrete reality: a Person whose voice is heard both in the created world and in the conscience.

Infallibility

During the 1860s, the campaign for declaring papal infallibility in matters of faith and morals was being fanatically pressed in English ultra-montane circles. Manning was backed up by another Oxford convert, W.G. Ward, who taught theology at the Westminster Seminary of St Edmund's, Ware. He was also editor of the *Dublin Review*, where his intemperate dismissal of all other views but his own exaggerated infallibilism irritated Newman among many others. Newman's friends kept writing to beg him to 'speak out', especially when a Council was called, which was to open in 1869, the first since the Council of Trent three hundred years earlier. Papal infallibility, not at first on the agenda, became a major issue for the First Vatican Council.

Newman could not see his way to making an intervention himself, since he was not in a position of authority, but he backed one of his younger Fathers, Ignatius Ryder, who carried on a pamphlet controversy with Ward. However, quite accidentally, Newman's views did come out, when a forceful letter of his to Ullathorne, deploring the speed of the drive towards a definition, was leaked to the press while the Council was actually in session. Although it created a public uproar, Newman was quite glad his views had come out even without his intention, and they did encourage the minority who argued against a definition. By their arguments they secured the moderations which made the final decree acceptable to the Church as a whole, and in fact, as Newman pointed out to distressed friends, actually limited the Pope's power in practice.

Many Catholics wrote to Newman, bewildered by what seemed an impossible new dogma, and he was able, by his knowledge of the history of the early Councils, to calm their fears. Popes had always acted as if their word was final in doctrinal controversies and they certainly shared in the gift of the Holy Spirit to the whole Church to guide it into all truth. All that the definition had done was to make clear the limits within which this power could be exercised; infallibility could no longer be claimed for every utterance of every Pope as Ward had sometimes seemed to insist. Something like this minimalist interpretation was put forward by the Roman theologian Fessler, who had been Secretary to the Council, and approved by the Pope himself. But this did not appear before a good deal of havoc had been caused by triumphalist ultras in countries where Catholics were in the minority.

In England, Gladstone wrote a best-selling pamphlet, furiously declaring that the definition had completely altered the ancient Catholic religion into something he called Vaticanism, which by turning the Pope into an infallible oracle had divided the allegiance of English Catholics from the Crown. An avalanche of letters descended on Newman, calling on him to answer. Newman felt he could now write on the subject of infallibility, because he would be defending Catholics against the charge of disloyalty by putting forward the moderate interpretation of the 'new' dogma in the context of the historical development of doctrine in the Church.

Newman's answer to Gladstone was published as a *Letter to the Duke of Norfolk*, because the young Duke (who had been at the Oratory School) was the premier Duke of England and also the premier Catholic layman. Under this dull title we find a masterly short essay on conscience and on authority, written in Newman's clearest style and treating papal infallibility in a reasonable way, by showing what it did not mean. Thus it helped to pacify the suspicious public, and even Gladstone, to a certain extent.

Newman was nearly seventy-four when the *Letter* came out in January 1875. Just before it he had lost several old friends, including the convert lawyer James Hope whom Newman had consulted on every venture. Then in May 1875 Ambrose St John suddenly became gravely ill, after heat-stroke. He died, just when he had seemed to be recovering, after some days of delirium. It was a terrible loss to Newman, who had relied so much on St John's loyal friendship and assistance in all the work of the Oratory. He had always expected

Ambrose to be his successor and executor. It was a strange fate that all his oldest friends had died before he was made a cardinal. In the meantime, in 1878, his old Oxford college, Trinity, made him their first Honorary Fellow. He visited Oxford to receive the honour, the first time he had set foot in the city since 1846.

The glorious last years

It was not till 1879, when Pius IX was succeeded by Leo XIII, that the cloud of suspicion was lifted forever. Newman was made a cardinal, partly at the request of English laymen, headed by the Duke of Norfolk. He was seventy-eight and beginning to grow frail, but he rose to the occasion, made a rousing speech in Rome for Christian truth against the liberal idea that religion was merely a matter of opinion, and came back to England to a series of grand receptions in London and Oxford.

Newman's final ten years were spent quietly, a serene old age in his beloved Oratory, with new novices coming in at last, and constant visitors. After a bad fall and illness in 1886 his physical strength and his sight began to fail and Fr Neville had to write his letters for him. He said his last Mass at Christmas 1889. In the summer he gained strength again and was present at the school prize giving, talking cheerfully to all visitors. But on 11th August, after barely two days confined to his bed, he died peacefully.

He was buried at the Oratory's cemetery at Rednal. A respectful crowd of fifteen to twenty thousand people watched his funeral cortège wind through

Birmingham, and he was praised and honoured in all the national newspapers which had once attacked him.

Cardinal Manning, who was to die only a few years later, was too frail to attend Cardinal Newman's funeral. But a week later, in front of a huge crowd gathered from all over Great Britain and Europe at a memorial service in the Brompton Oratory, Manning gave a moving eulogy.

If any proof were needed of the immeasurable work that he has wrought in England, the last week would be enough. Who could doubt that a great multitude of his personal friends in the first half of his life, and a still greater multitude of those who have been instructed, consoled and won to God by the unequalled beauty and irresistible persuasion of his writings – who could doubt that they, at such a time as this, would pour out the love and gratitude of their hearts? But that the public voice of England, political and religious, in all its diversities, should for once unite in love and veneration of a man who had broken through its sacred barriers and defied its religious prejudices, who could have believed it? He had committed the hitherto unpardonable sin in England. He had rejected the whole Tudor Settlement in religion. He had become Catholic as our fathers were. And yet for no one in our memory has such a heartfelt and loving veneration been poured out. Of this, one proof is enough. Someone has said, whether Rome canonises him or not, he will be canonised in the thoughts of pious people of many creeds in England.

The legacy of Cardinal Newman

In letters and memoranda, both Newman's own and those of other people, we can discover a strong, active, humorous and sympathetic character. The child who "wished the Arabian Tales were true" and thought angels were hiding from him, is the same boy who made a kite with glass eyes and at school formed a club, writing most of its magazine *The Spy*, himself (based on the *Spectator*). Wishing for opposition, he had to provide it himself, writing the *Anti-Spy* as well. He was a physically active boy, bathing often in the river, and once he tried to row round the Isle of Wight in a fog. All his life he was an indefatigable walker; as a young don at Oriel he went out riding with Hurrell Froude and other friends.

Newman the pastor

People who only know Newman through the *Apologia* can get a distorted idea of his character, as if he never did anything but think and write. When writing of his Oxford days he includes nothing about his active pastoral life, visiting the sick and dying, baptising and marrying parishioners as well as preaching the famous sermons – many, as he recorded, "to empty benches" because the authorities altered the time of dinner in college halls to prevent the young men attending them. This active pastoral life he continued as a Catholic priest, and in later years, as his community dwindled, he undertook more rather than less of the duty. Preaching to factory workers, Irish immigrants, tradesmen and a few professional people, hearing their confessions, saying and singing the masses – all this filled his days, year after year. Something of this can be gleaned from his diaries and from reminiscences of Oratory parishioners, who held him in great affection and kept cuttings of his hair (got from the hairdresser) and pieces of his clothes. "Father knows well how to speak of the cross," one old woman said. And one girl recalled how he had come out of the confessional to comfort her when she began to cry at her first confession.

As well as to the wives and widows of friends, Newman's friendship extended to a number of single women. Maria Giberne, who knew him in his youth and followed him into the Church, eventually became a nun in France and Newman was still corresponding with her into their eighties, giving her down-to-earth advice about digestion in old age: "You are not an ostrich. I am serious." Emily Bowles, who also first met Newman at Littlemore, later lived in London, prison visiting, among other good works, recorded that Newman made her accept £5 for "charitable boots and umbrellas" worn out in this voluntary service.

Early in the 1860s, during that difficult time before the *Apologia*, Emily Bowles visited Newman at the Birmingham Oratory after a lapse of seven years. She left us a vivid description which encapsulates the spirit of the man as he shouldered his cross. "The brightness that lit up that worn face as he received me at the door, carrying in several packages himself." She was shocked by his appearance: "His grand massive face was scored with lines of intense grief, disappointment and the patient bearing up against the failure of hope.

Whenever he spoke, the expression softened…" Later, after the abortive Oxford affair, which she knew about from London gossip, he called to see her and she asked him when "all these secret doings might be told from the housetops: and he, with that peculiarly brightening, yet sad smile that about that time of his life was most touching, replied, 'My dear child! My dear child! When I am gone.'"

The romantic realist and the Christian revelation

Newman never looked for an ideal Church. He had always looked at the fact of the Church in history, and it was only when he became convinced that the Church of England was no longer an integral part of the One Holy Catholic and Apostolic Church that he submitted to the Holy See as "the divinely appointed centre of unity." He never lost this conviction of the central unifying role of the Papacy, though his knowledge of history led him to take the moderate view of the Pope's powers held by most of the English bishops.

Personal sanctity

However frustrated Newman might sometimes have felt within the Church as institution, he was always able to take refuge in the real presence of Christ. Though he distrusted emotional "spirituality" there are references to be found in the letters of various people to the impression he made, as a person and as a priest, of simple holiness. Lady Lothian, a new convert in 1851, was nervous of meeting him but was soon put at ease. "That which struck me most was his childlike sympathy and humility," she wrote, "and next to that the vivid clearness with which he gives an opinion… His saying of Mass is most striking. I do not know what makes the difference, but one is conscious of a difference. It appeared to me very unearthly."

Thirty-odd years later, in 1882, Lord Chief Justice Coleridge (son of the Judge who had lectured Newman on his moral deterioration in 1853) wrote to a friend,

> I cannot analyse it or explain it, but to this hour he awes me like no other man I ever saw. He is as simple and humble and playful as a child, and yet, I am with a being unlike anyone else. He lifts me up for a time, and subdues me…"

In 1886 Newman stayed in London with Dean Church, who wrote to the Warden of Keble College, "He was so bright, so kind, so affectionate; very old, and soon tired, but also soon refreshed with a pause of rest, and making fun of his old age. 'You know I could not do an addition sum.'"

In everyday life Newman had an acute and shrewd sense of humour, which appears in his letters, even in letters which comment on current anxieties and annoyances. Newman was remarkably resilient and in the context of faith ever hopeful. Confident that God would bring order out of chaos in his own good time: "He knows what he is about." This phrase actually comes from a meditation on God's care for every person's life and development, through every trial and perplexity. "Therefore, I will trust him. Whatever, wherever I am, I can never be thrown away."

Newman's mission

Newman did not become a theologian in the conventional sense, but dealt with modern problems of faith based on an historical study of theology, which is why he has exercised such an influence on Catholic theologians in Europe and America. But everything that Newman wrote was intended for any intelligent reader. He told one correspondent that he had written the last hundred pages of *The Grammar of Assent* "especially for such ladies as are bullied by infidels and do not know how to answer them – a misfortune which I fear is not rare in this day." It draws out from history and from the universal experience of moral obligation the accumulating probabilities that Christianity is a true revelation from the divine Creator of all things. Final acceptance is an act of will and duty, and faith in it, since it comes from God, is certain, but it cannot be freely accepted till it is seen to be reasonable and worthy of credence. Newman once said that this was the way both factory girls and philosophers were converted. It was less a theory than a diagnosis of experience.

John Henry Cardinal Newman stands as a beacon of sanity and prudence, an apostle to those assailed by doubt, a friend for those who are tempted to impatience or despair, a saint for all the people that he himself cared for whilst on this earth.

Newman's Beatification and Canonisation

The Cause

During Newman's lifetime there were many who regarded him as a saint. Father Bernard Dalgairns, to take a particularly significant example, reported to Father Faber his final interview with Newman before departing to join the London Oratory: "His eyes looked then just like a saint's and he spoke and acted like one, so disinterestedly, so gently." At Newman's death the ultra-Protestant *Evangelical Magazine* declared that of all the saints "in the Roman calendar there are very few that can be considered better entitled to that designation than Cardinal Newman". However, the Birmingham Oratory, bearing in mind the dictum of St Philip Neri, "to love to be unknown", that was so dear to Newman himself, was reluctant to push his Cause. And it was not until 1941 that an American Dominican, Fr Charles Callan, called for the Cause to be opened in an article in *America Magazine*. Then in 1942 the Archbishop of Toronto, in response to the overwhelmingly positive response, gave his imprimatur to the first prayer for Newman's canonisation. Finally, in England itself the Newman scholar Mgr H. Francis Davis gave his support in an article in 1952. Six years later the Archbishop of Birmingham opened the Cause, and a year later set up an historical commission to examine the evidence.

However, it was not until 1986 that a reconstituted historical commission completed the necessary documentation to conclude the diocesan process. This was then sent to Rome to the Congregation for the Causes of Saints, which subsequently confirmed the conclusion reached by the commission. Accordingly, on 22nd January 1991, Pope John Paul II declared Newman to be 'Venerable' or a figure to be venerated for the 'heroic virtues' that he displayed in his life. The formal recognition by the Pope of Newman as 'Venerable' still required divine confirmation in order for him to reach the next rung, so to speak, in the ladder to sainthood, that of beatification.

Although there had never been the kind of popular cult of Newman the theologian and writer that a figure like Mother Teresa inspired with her works of heroic charity, over the years the belief that Newman was a saint had been growing all over the Catholic world. As a result, more and more people were praying for his intercession. And then on 15th August 2001, the feast of the Assumption of the Blessed Virgin Mary, an American living in Marshfield near Boston, who was training for the married diaconate, was inexplicably cured of a severe spinal disorder that had left him bent doubled over. Jack Sullivan claimed it was the result of his seeking in prayer the intercession of Newman, ever since watching a television interview a year previously in June 2000. Thereupon the Archdiocese of Boston established a tribunal that interviewed witnesses and collected all the evidence available, which was then forwarded to the Congregation for the Causes of Saints in Rome in November 2006. On 24th April 2008 the medical consultants at the Congregation unanimously agreed that they could not find any natural explanation for the cure. On 23rd April 2009 the Congregation's theological consultants unanimously recognised Jack Sullivan's recovery as a miracle. Pope Benedict XVI decreed on 3rd July 2009 that Newman be beatified. On 19th September 2010 he beatified Newman at Cofton Park in Birmingham, during his visit to England.

Twelve years later on 15th May 2013 another American living in Chicago, Melissa Villalobos, had become interested in Newman after watching a programme about him. The expectant mother was bleeding dangerously from a partially detached placenta, for which there was no medication or medical treatment but only the possibility of healing after resting in bed for a considerable amount of time. One morning she began to bleed even more seriously. She desperately prayed, "Please Cardinal Newman make the bleeding stop!" Thereupon the bleeding immediately stopped. Following the same kind of investigation that was carried out in the case of Jack Sullivan, Pope Francis decreed on 13th February 2019 that Newman would be canonised. His feast day is 9th October.

In clear anticipation of the beatification, the Congregation for the Causes of Saints had already instructed that Newman's remains should be exhumed, to allow for their public veneration in accordance with usual Catholic practice. It was then discovered that Newman had been buried in a wooden coffin that, along with his remains, had entirely decomposed in the damp soil, apart from a brass plate (with his name and date of death), the brass handles with some bits of cloth attached, a brass replica of his cardinal's hat, and a wooden crucifix inlaid in silver. This discovery had no implications for the beatification, only for the projected public veneration. One is tempted to feel that Newman's 'disappearance' from this earth was his final fulfilment of the maxim of St Philip Neri, the founder of the Congregation of the Oratory, which he so cherished: *amare nesciri*, 'to love not to be known'. Indeed, the 20th August 1890 report in *The Birmingham Daily Post* of Newman's funeral and burial ended:

> and then the coffin was covered with mould of a softer texture than the marly [clay and lime] stratum in which the grave is cut. This was done in studious and affectionate fulfilment of a desire of Dr Newman's which some may deem fanciful, but which sprang from his reverence for the letter of the Divine Word; which, as he conceived, enjoins us to facilitate rather than impede the operation of the law "Dust thou art, and unto dust shalt thou return."

Statue of John Henry Newman installed outside the London Oratory

Portrait of John Henry Newman by William Charles Ross, circa 1845

Oriel College, Oxford, where Newman was a fellow from 1822

University Church of St Mary the Virgin in Oxford, Newman's first parish

Newman's private chapel in the Birmingham Oratory

Newman's study and private chapel in the Birmingham Oratory

Newman's writing desk in his private study

Desk in Newman's personal library where he wrote his most famous work, *Apologia pro Vita Sua*

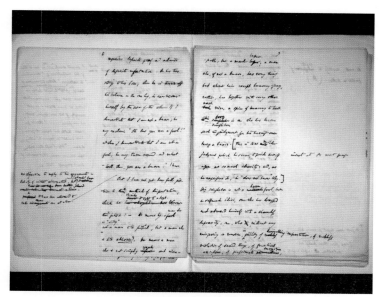

Original manuscript of *Apologia pro Vita Sua*

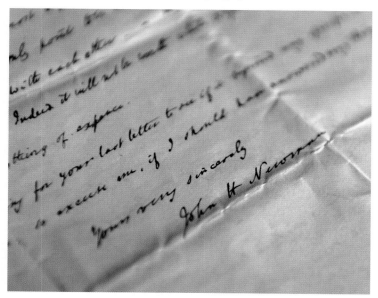

Letter from John Henry Newman to Cardinal Manning

Cardinal Newman's biretta in his private rooms in the Birmingham Oratory

Clerical chasubles worn by Newman for use at Mass

Glasses worn by Cardinal Newman among his personal effects

Shaving razor blade belonging to Cardinal Newman with inscription
'The Very Rev Father Newman'

Newman's personal rosary

Portrait of Cardinal Newman by Lady Coleridge (née Seymour), 1876

Interior of the Birmingham Oratory church

Personal chalice used by
Cardinal Newman

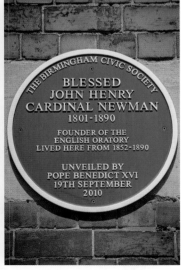

Plaque of Cardinal Newman installed
for his beatification in 2010

Cardinal Newman's travelling hat

A selection of Cardinal Newman's shoes

Portrait of Cardinal Newman by Emmeline Deane, circa 1884

The grave of Cardinal Newman in Rednal Cemetery

Bust of Newman in the cloister of the Birmingham Oratory Church

Relic casket of John Henry Newman

Reliquary in the Birmingham Oratory containing the hair of Cardinal Newman, one of the few relics from the saint's body itself

PART II

SELECTIONS FROM
NEWMAN'S WRITINGS

John Henry Newman's writings are very voluminous. He was not primarily a systematic thinker, but instead addressed particular questions for particular audiences. Nevertheless, he did have a coherent and persuasive understanding of the Christian faith, which informed all of his mature writing and preaching. Various scholars have attempted to summarise this, using extracts from his writings. The short summary that follows, in the first part of this section, is abridged from a booklet called *The Mind of Cardinal Newman*, compiled by Fr Charles Dessain (editor of Newman's letters) and first published by CTS in 1974.

The second part adds some reflections drawn from another CTS booklet, *Daily Christian Living with John Henry Newman* (2009), which itself abridges a selection edited by Joyce Sugg in the CTS *Guides to Holiness* series (1987).

Lastly, to give an idea of how Newman writes at length, we have printed in full three of his sermons, which were first reprinted in CTS pamphlet form over a hundred years ago.

Abbreviations for Newman's Works

Apo. *Apologia pro Vita Sua;* **Ari.** *The Arians of the Fourth Century;* **Ath. I, II** *Select Treatises of St Athanasius;* **D.A.** *Discussions and Arguments on Various Subjects;* **Dev.** *An Essay on the Development of Christian Doctrine;* **Diff. I, II** *Certain Difficulties Felt by Anglicans in Catholic Teaching;* **Ess. I, II** *Essays Critical and Historical;* **G.A.** *An Essay in Aid of a Grammar of Assent;* **H.S. I, II, III** *Historical Sketches;* **Idea** *The Idea of a University Defined and Illustrated;* **Jfc.** *Lectures on the Doctrine of Justification;* **Med.** *Meditations and Devotions;* **Mix.** *Discourses Addressed to Mixed Congregations;* **O.S.** *Sermons Preached on Various Occasions;* **P.S. I–VIII** *Parochial and Plain Sermons;* **Prepos.** *Present Position of Catholics;* **S.D.** *Sermons Bearing on Subjects of the Day;* **T.T.** *Tracts Theological and Ecclesiastical;* **U.S.** *Fifteen Sermons Preached before the University of Oxford.*

A Summary of Newman's Thought

1. The Experience of Conscience

Conscience is not a long-sighted selfishness, nor a desire to be consistent with oneself; but it is a messenger from him, who, both in nature and in grace, speaks to us behind a veil, and teaches and rules us by his representatives. Conscience is the aboriginal Vicar of Christ.

The supremacy of conscience. Diff. II, 248

I feel myself in his presence. He says to me, "Do this: don't do that". You may tell me that this dictate is a mere law of my nature, as is to joy or to grieve. I cannot understand this. No, it is the echo of a person speaking to me. Nothing shall persuade me that it does not ultimately proceed from a person external to me. It carries with it its proof of its divine origin. My nature feels towards it as towards a person. When I obey it, I feel a satisfaction; when I disobey, a soreness – just like that which I feel in pleasing or offending some revered friend.

A description of conscience. Diff. II, 314

2. Conscience Leads to God

Were it not for this voice, speaking so clearly in my conscience and my heart, I should be an atheist, or a pantheist or a polytheist when I looked into the world. I am speaking for myself only; and I am far from denying the real force of the arguments in proof of a God, drawn from the general facts of human society and the course of history, but these do not warm or enlighten me.

Fidelity to conscience is the way to truth. Apo. 241

Thus conscience is a connecting principle between the creature and his Creator; and the firmest hold of theological truths is gained by habits of personal religion...Then they are brought into his presence as that of a living Person, and are able to hold converse with him, and that with a directness and simplicity, with a confidence and intimacy... so that it is doubtful whether we realise the company of our fellow-men with greater keenness than these favoured minds are able to contemplate and adore the unseen, incomprehensible Creator.

A purified and sensitivised mind is needed. G.A. 117-18

The more a person tries to obey his conscience, the more he gets alarmed at himself, for obeying it so imperfectly ... But next, while he thus grows in self-knowledge, he also understands more and more clearly that the voice of conscience has nothing gentle, nothing of mercy in its tone. It is severe and even stern. It does not speak of forgiveness but of punishment. It suggests to him a future judgement; it does not tell him how he can avoid it.

Those advance who are dissatisfied with themselves. O.S. 67

The guide of life, implanted in our nature, discriminating right from wrong, and investing right with authority and sway, is our conscience, which revelation does but enlighten, strengthen and refine. Coming from one and the same Author, these internal and external monitors of course recognise and bear witness to each other.

Conscience bows to the voice of God in revelation. H.S. III, 79

3. We are Made for a God who Loves us

You see the educated man, full of thought, full of intelligence, full of action, but still with a stone heart, as cold and dead as regards his affections, as if he were the poor ignorant countryman. You see others, with warm affections, perhaps, for their families, with benevolent feelings towards their fellow-men, yet stopping there; centreing their hearts on what is sure to fail them, as being perishable. Life passes, riches fly away, popularity is fickle, the senses decay, the world changes, friends die. One alone is constant; one alone is true to us; one alone can be all things to us!

God all in all. P.S. V, 324–26

In all circumstances of joy or sorrow, hope or fear, let us aim at having him in our utmost heart; let us have no secret apart from him. Let us acknowledge him as throned within us at the very springs of thought and affection.

Whole-hearted love. P.S. V, 236

We know that no temper of mind is acceptable in the Divine Presence without love: it is love which makes Christian fear differ from servile dread, and true faith differ from the faith of devils: yet in the beginning of the religious life, fear is the prominent evangelical grace, and love is but latent in fear, and has in course of time to be developed out of what seems its contradictory. Then when it is developed, it takes that prominent place which fear held before, yet protecting not superseding it.

The place of fear in the Christian life. Dev. 420

Let a person who trusts he is on the whole serving God acceptably, look back upon his past life, and he will find how critical were moments and acts, which at the time seemed the most indifferent: as for instance the school he was sent to as a child, the occasion of his falling in with those persons who have most benefited him, the accidents which determined his calling or his prospects, whatever they were. God's hand is ever over his own, and he leads them forward by ways they know not of.

Trust in God's loving care. P.S. IV, 261

4. Our Need of Clearer Teaching

The sense of right and wrong, which is the first element in religion, is so delicate, so fitful, so easily puzzled, obscured, perverted so biased by pride and passion, so unsteady in its course, that, in the struggle for existence amid the various exercises and triumphs of the human intellect this sense is at once the highest of all teachers, yet the least luminous.

Revelation is the supply of an urgent demand. Diff. II, 253-54

One of the greatest of the perplexities of nature is this very one, that the Creator should have left you to yourselves. You know there is a God, yet you know your own ignorance of him, of his will, of your duties, of your prospects. A revelation would be the greatest of possible boons that could be vouchsafed to you. After all you do not know, you only conclude that there is a God; you see him not, you do but hear of him. He acts under a veil; he is on the point of manifesting himself to you at every turn, yet he does not. He has impressed on your hearts anticipations of his majesty; in every part of creation has he left traces of his presence and given glimpses of his glory.

There is the strongest presumption that our Creator has not left us to ourselves. Mix. 276-77

The common sense of mankind ... feels that the very idea of revelation implies a present informant and guide, and that an infallible one; not a mere abstract declaration of Truths unknown before to man, or a record of history, or the result of an antiquarian research, but a message and a lesson speaking to this man and that ... We are told that God has spoken. Where? In a book? We have tried it and it disappoints; it disappoints us, that holy and most blessed gift, not from any fault of its own, but because it is used for a purpose for which it was not given. The Ethiopian's reply, when St Philip asked him if he understood what he was reading, is the voice of nature; "How can I, unless some man shall guide me?" The Church undertakes that office.

We need clear guidance. Dev. 87–88

5. The Way to Faith

Our most natural mode of reasoning is, not from propositions to propositions, but from things to things, from concrete to concrete, from wholes to wholes. This is the mode in which we ordinarily reason, dealing with things directly, and as they stand ... and it is especially exemplified both in uneducated men, and in men of genius.

> *The shepherd can tell the weather, the good man can grasp religious truth.* G.A. 330–31

Here, then, are two processes, distinct from each other, the original process of reasoning, and next the process of investigating our reasonings. All men reason, for to reason is nothing more than to gain truth from former truth ... but all men do not reflect upon their own reasonings, much less reflect truly and accurately, so as to do justice to their own meaning; but only in proportion to their abilities and attainments. In other words, all men have a reason, but not all men can give a reason.

> *Our reason, left to work naturally, tells us to believe.* U.S. 258–59

True faith is what may be called colourless, like air or water; it is but the medium through which the soul sees Christ; and the soul as little really rests upon it and contemplates it, as the eye can see the air. When, then, men are bent on holding it (as it were) in their hands ... they substitute for it a feeling, notion, sentiment, conviction, or act of reason, which they may hang over, and dote upon. They rather aim at experiences (as they are called) within them, than at him that is without them.

Loving faith leads to Christ. It may be 'blind' and without feeling. Jfc. 336

From the age of fifteen, dogma has been the fundamental principle of my religion: I know no other religion; I cannot enter into the idea of any other sort of religion; religion, as a mere sentiment, is to me a dream and a mockery. As well can there be filial love without the fact of a father, as devotion without the fact of a Supreme Being.

Newman's own testimony. Apo. 49

6. The Purpose of Creeds and Dogmas

We must know concerning God, before we can feel love, fear, hope, or trust towards him. Devotion must have its objects: those objects, as being supernatural, when not represented to our senses by material symbols, must be set before the mind in propositions. The formula, which embodies a dogma for the theologian, readily suggests an object for the worshipper.

Faith seeks to understand. G.A. 120-21

If Christianity be an universal religion, suited not simply to one locality or period, but to all times and places, it cannot but vary in its relations and dealings towards the world around it, that is, it will develop.

In a higher world it is otherwise, but here below to be perfect is to have changed often. Dev. 58

Christianity is eminently an objective religion. For the most part it tells us of persons and facts in simple words, and leaves that announcement to produce its effect on such hearts as are prepared to receive it.

How revealed religion works. Diff. II, 86-87

The articles of the Creed are brief enunciations and specimens of some, and of the chief, of the great mercies vouchsafed to man in the Gospel. They are truths of pregnant significance, and of direct practical bearing on Christian life and conduct. Such, for instance, obviously is "one baptism for the remission of sins," and "the resurrection of the body". Such then must be our profession of "catholicity". And, thus considered, the two, "the Catholic Church" and "the Communion of Saints", certainly suggest an explanation of each other; the one introducing us to our associates and patrons in heaven, and the other pointing out to us where to find the true teaching and the means of grace on earth.

The Creeds are light in darkness. Ath. II, 65

7. The Church Protects the Revealed Message

If the Church, initiated in the apostles and continued in their successors, has been set up for the direct object of protecting, preserving, and declaring the revelation, and that by means of the guardianship and providence of its Divine Author, we are led on to perceive that, in asserting this, we are in other words asserting, that, so far as the message entrusted to it is concerned, the Church is infallible.

We need a guarantee for the present day. Diff. II, 323

The Catholic people, in the length and breadth of Christendom, were the obstinate champions of Catholic truth, and the bishops were not ... Perhaps it was permitted, in order to impress upon the Church ... the great evangelical lesson, that, not the wise and powerful, but the obscure, the unlearned, and the weak constitute her real strength.

The Church is a communion, and consists of all its members. Ari. 445–46

Go through the long annals of Church history, century after century, and say, was there ever a time when her bishops ... forgot that they had a message to deliver to the world − not the task merely of administering spiritual consolation, or of making the sick-bed easy, or of training up good members of society, or of 'serving tables' (though all this was included in their range of duty) − but specially and directly, a definite message to high and low, from the world's Maker, whether men would hear or whether they would forbear?

The Church's mission. Diff. II, 197

The structure of Scripture is such, so irregular and unmethodical, that either we must hold that the Gospel doctrine or message is not contained in Scripture (and if so, either that there was no message at all given, or that it is given elsewhere, external to Scripture), or, as the alternative, we must hold that it is but indirectly and covertly recorded there, that is, under the surface.

Why, for instance, should a certain number of letters, more or less private, written by St Paul and others to particular persons or bodies, contain the whole of what the Holy Spirit taught them? ... They did not sit down with a design to commit to paper all they had to say on the whole subject, all they could say about the Gospel.

The word of God contains the revealed message but is not self-sufficient. D.A. 142, 148

8. The Church, Visible and Invisible

(In) the Catholic Church ... I recognised at once a reality which was quite a new thing with me. Then I was sensible that I was not making for myself a Church by an effort of thought; I needed not to make an act of faith in her; I had not painfully to force myself into a position, but my mind fell back upon itself in relaxation and in peace, and I gazed at her almost passively as a great objective fact. I looked at her; at her rites, her ceremonial, and her precepts; and I said, "This is a religion".

Cardinal Newman's reaction on becoming a Catholic. Apo. 339-40

Everyone who desires unity, who prays for it, who endeavours to further it, who witnesses for it, who behaves Christianly towards the members of Churches alienated from us, who is at amity with them (saving his duty to his own communion and to the truth itself), who tries to edify them, while he edifies himself and his own people, may surely be considered, as far as he himself is concerned, as breaking down the middle wall of division, and renewing the ancient bonds of unity and concord by the power of charity.

We must work and pray for unity. Ess. II, 374

This then is the special glory of the Christian Church, that its members do not depend merely on what is visible, they are not mere stones of a building, piled one on another, and bound together from without, but they are one and all the births and manifestations of one and the same unseen spiritual principle or power, 'living stones', internally connected, as branches from a tree, not as the parts of a heap. They are members of the Body of Christ.... So that in a true sense it may be said, that from the day of Pentecost to this hour there has been in the Church but one Holy One, the King of kings, and Lord of lords himself, who is in all believers, and through whom they are what they are; their separate persons being but as separate developments, vessels, instruments, and works of him who is invisible.

We are members of Christ and members one of another. P.S. IV, 170

The Church is a collection of souls, brought together in one by God's secret grace, though that grace comes to them through visible instruments, and unites them to a visible hierarchy. What is seen, is not the whole of the Church, but the visible part of it. When we say that Christ loves his Church, we mean that he loves, nothing of earthly nature, but the fruit of his own grace ... in innumerable hearts.

The invisible part of the Church. O.S. 57

9. Father, Son, and Holy Spirit, One God

Let it be observed the mystery lies, not in any one of the statements which constitute the doctrine, but in their combination. The meaning of each proposition is on a level with our understanding. There is no intellectual difficulty in approaching any one of them. "God is a Father; God is a Son; God is a Holy Spirit: The Father is not the Son; The Son is not the Holy Ghost; the Holy Ghost is not the Father; God is numerically One; there are not three Gods." In which of these propositions do we not sufficiently understand what is meant to be told us? For devotion, then ... the mystery is no difficulty.

We contemplate each proposition separately and find motives for devotion and faithful obedience. Ath. II, 316-17

That there was but one First Principle of all things was a fundamental doctrine of all Catholics ... Christianity taught a Divine Trinity: how was this consistent? ... Catholic theologians met this difficulty, both before and after the Nicene Council, by insisting on the unity of origin, which they taught as existing in the Divine

Triad, the Son and the Spirit having a communicated divinity from the Father, and a personal unity with him … It was for the same reason that the Father was called God absolutely, while the Second and Third Persons were designated by their personal names of 'the Son', or 'the Word', and 'the Holy Ghost'; viz. because they are to be regarded, not as separated from, but as inherent in the Father.

From the Father proceed the Son and the Holy Spirit. T.T. 167–69

If we wish to express the sacred Mystery of the Incarnation accurately, we should rather say that God is man, than that man is God. Not that the latter proposition is not altogether Catholic in its wording, but the former expresses the history of the economy (if I may so call it) and confines Our Lord's personality to his divine nature, making his manhood an adjunct; whereas to say that man is God, does the contrary of both of these – leads us to consider him a man primarily and personally, with some vast and unknown dignity super-added.

We wish to preserve the pure truth of Revelation. Ess. I, 74

10. Our Lord and Saviour

Before he came on earth, he had but the perfections
of God, but afterwards he had also the virtues of a
creature, such as faith, meekness, self-denial. Before he
came on earth he could not be tempted to evil; but
afterwards he had a man's heart, and a man's wants
and infirmities. His divine nature indeed pervaded his
manhood, so that every deed and word of his in the
flesh savoured of eternity and infinity; but on the other
hand, from the time he was born of the Virgin Mary,
he had a natural fear of danger, a natural shrinking
from pain, though ever subject to the ruling influence
of that holy and eternal Essence which was in him.

The Son of God is truly man. P.S. III, 166

Persons influence us, voices melt us, looks subdue us,
deeds inflame us. Many a man will live and die upon
a dogma: no man will be a martyr for a conclusion.

The words apply to the life of Our Lord. D.A. 293

It is the very idea that he is God, which gives a meaning to his sufferings; what is to me a man, and nothing more, in agony, or scourged, or crucified? There are many holy martyrs, and their torments were terrible. But here I see one dropping blood, gashed by the thong and stretched upon the cross, and he is God. It is no tale of human woe which I am reading here; it is the record of the passion of the great Creator.

We must realise what God has done for our sake. Mix. 321

11. The Gift of the Spirit

We are able to see that the Saviour, when once he entered into this world, never so departed as to suffer things to be as they were before he came; for he is still with us, not in mere gifts, but by the substitution of his Spirit for himself, and that, both in the Church, and in the souls of individual Christians.

> *Ever since he was glorified Christ has been giving his Spirit.*
> P.S. II, 221

A true Christian, then, may almost be defined as one who has a ruling sense of God's presence within him. As none but justified persons have that privilege, so none but the justified have that practical perception of it. A true Christian, or one who is in a state of acceptance with God, is he, who, in such sense, has faith in him, as to live in the thought that he is present with him – present not externally, not in nature merely, or in providence, but in his innermost heart, or in his conscience.

> *God dwells in the centre of the soul and there the good*
> *Christian must find him.* P.S. V, 225-26

12. The Mass and the Sacraments

Though he now sits on the right hand of God, he has, in one sense, never left the world since he first entered it: for by the ministration of the Holy Ghost, he is really with us in an unknown way, and ever imparts himself to those who seek him ... And as he is still with us, for all that he is in heaven, so, again, is the hour of his cross and passion ever mystically present, through it he past these eighteen hundred years. Time and space have no portion in the spiritual Kingdom, which he has founded; and the rites of his Church are as mysterious spells by which he annuls them both ... Thus Christ shines through them, as through transparent bodies, without impediment ... He has touched them, and breathed upon them, when he ordained them; and thenceforth they have a virtue residing in them.

Christ reaches us today through his sacraments. P.S. III, 277–78

How many are the souls, in distress, anxiety or loneliness, whose one need is to find a being to whom they can pour out their feelings unheard by the world?

Tell them out they must; they cannot tell them out to those whom they see every hour. They want to tell them and not to tell them; and they want to tell them out, yet be as if they be not told; they wish to tell them out to one strong enough to bear them, yet not too strong to despise them; they wish to tell them to one who can at once advise and can sympathise with them; they wish to relieve themselves of a load, to gain a solace. If there is a heavenly idea in the Catholic Church, looking at it simply as an idea, surely, next after the Blessed Sacrament, confession is such.

There is a constant invitation to repent and begin afresh.
Prepos. 351

At times we seem to catch a glimpse of a form which we shall hereafter see face to face. We approach, and in spite of the darkness, our hands, or our head, or our brow, or our lips become, as it were, sensible of the contact of something more than earthly. We know not where we are, but we have been bathing in water, and a voice tells us that it is blood. Or we have a mark signed upon our foreheads, and it spake of Calvary. Or we recollect a hand laid upon our heads, and surely it had the print of nails in it, and resembled his who with a touch gave sight to the blind and raised the dead. Or we have been eating and drinking; and it was not a dream surely, that one fed us from his wounded side, and renewed our nature by the heavenly meat he gave.

We may even experience Christ's presence in his sacraments.
P.S. V, 10–11

81

13. The Reality of Sin

To consider the world in its length and breadth, its various history, the many races of man, their starts, their fortunes, their mutual alienation, their conflicts ... the greatness and littleness of man, his far-reaching aims, his short duration ... the prevalence and intensity of sin, the pervading idolatries, the corruptions, the dreary hopeless irreligion – all this is a vision to dizzy and appall; and inflicts on the mind a profound mystery, which is absolutely beyond human solution.

What shall be said to this head-piercing, reason-bewildering fact? I can only answer, that either there is no creator, or this living society of man is in a true sense discarded from his presence ... if there is a God, since there is a God, the human race is implicated in some terrible aboriginal calamity. It is out of joint with the purpose of its Creator. This is a fact, a fact as true as the fact of its existence; and thus the doctrine of what is theologically called original sin becomes to me almost as certain as that the world exists, and as the existence of God.

Man is called so high and falls so low. Apo. 241–43

The Church aims, not at making a show, but at doing a work. She regards this world, and all that is in it, as a mere shadow, as dust and ashes, compared with the value of one single soul. She holds that, unless she can, in her own way, do good to souls, it is no use her doing anything; she holds that it were better for sun and moon to drop from heaven, for the earth to fail, and for all the many millions who are upon it to die of starvation in extremest agony, so far as temporal affliction goes, than that one soul, I will not say, should be lost, but should commit one single venial sin, should tell one wilful untruth, though it harmed no one, or steal one poor farthing without excuse.

Deliberately to offend God is the greatest of all evils.
Diff. I, 239-40

14. Detachment, Surrender and Joy

To be detached is to be loosened from every tie which binds the soul to the earth, to be dependent on nothing sublunary, to lean on nothing temporal; it is to care simply nothing what other men choose to think or say of us, or do to us; to go about our own work, because it is our duty... without a care of the consequences; to account credit, honour, name, easy circumstances, comfort, human affections, just nothing at all, when any religious obligation involves the sacrifice of them.

Ready to sell everything in order to buy the pearl of great price.
H.S. III, 130

What then is it that we who profess religion lack? I repeat it, this: a willingness to be changed, a willingness to suffer ... Almighty God to change us. We do not like to let go our old selves ... But when a man comes to God to be saved, then, I say, the essence of true conversion is a surrender of himself, an unreserved, unconditional surrender.

To those who give up everything for him, God gives himself.
P.S. V, 241

Gloom is no Christian temper; that repentance is not real, which has not love in it; that self-chastisement is not acceptable, which is not sweetened by faith and cheerfulness. We must live in sunshine, even when in sorrow; we must live in God's presence, we must not shut ourselves up in our own hearts, even when we are reckoning up our past sins.

Our sadness is turned into joy. P.S. V, 271

The foundations of the ocean, the vast realms of water which girdle the earth, are as tranquil and as silent in the storm as in a calm. So it is with the souls of holy men. They have a well of peace springing up within them unfathomable; and though the accidents of the hour may make them seem agitated, yet in their hearts they are not so.

The underlying serenity of the true Christian. P.S. V, 69

15. The Prayer of Christians

This habit of prayer then, recurrent prayer, morning, noon, and night, is one discriminating point in Scripture Christianity, as arising from the text ... "our conversation is in heaven". In a word, there was no barrier, no cloud, no earthly object, interposed between the soul of the primitive Christian and its Saviour and Redeemer.

Prayer follows belief in a present God. S.D. 281

Everyone knows, who has any knowledge of the Gospel, that prayer is one of its special ordinances; but not everyone, perhaps, has noticed what kind of prayer its inspired teachers most carefully enjoying ... Yet it is observable, that though prayer for self is the first and plainest of Christian duties, the apostles especially insist on another kind of prayer; prayer for others, for ourselves with others, for the Church, and the world, that it may be brought into the Church. Intercession is the characteristic of Christian worship.

In prayer we show our love for others and their needs.
P.S. III, 350

Christians could not correspond; they could not combine; but they could pray for one another. Even their public prayers partook of this character of intercession; for to pray for the welfare of the whole Church was in fact a prayer for all classes of men and all individuals of which it was composed. It was in prayer that the Church was founded.

> *Our Lady and the apostles persevered with one mind in prayer.*
> Diff. II, 69

16. Purity and Influence

There is a famous instance of a holy man of old times, who, before his conversion, felt indeed the excellence of purity, but could not get himself to say more in prayer than "Give me chastity, but not yet". I will not be inconsiderate enough to make light of the power of temptation of any kind, nor will I presume to say that Almighty God will certainly shield a man from temptation for his wishing it; but whenever men complain, as they often do, of the arduousness of a high virtue, at least it were well that they should first ask themselves the question, whether they desire to have it. We hear much in this day of the impossibility of heavenly purity... are you sure that the impossibility which you insist upon does not lie, not in nature, but in the will? Let us but will, and our nature is changed "according to the power that worketh in us"... We dare not trust ourselves on the waters, though Christ bids us.

> *What you are from not desiring a gift, this you make*
> *an excuse for not possessing it.* P.S. V, 349-50

It should be recollected that there is no one, to speak in general terms, but is the better for occasional retreats from the world; and the more active and useful is a man's life, the greater is his need of them. But the occasional retirement of the many requires the lifelong retirement of the few, and an establishment of recluses is but the sanctuary of the un-cloistered. To be shut out from the world is their very duty to the world; to be in leisure is their business.

One of the benefits of monasteries. Ess. II, 419

17. The Blessed Virgin Mary

Mary is exalted for the sake of Jesus. It was fitting that she, as being a creature, though the first of creatures, should have an office of ministration. She, as others, came into the world to do a work, she had a mission to fulfil; her grace and her glory are not for her own sake, but for her Maker's; and to her is committed the custody of the Incarnation her glories and the devotion paid her proclaim and define the right faith concerning him as God and man.

Mary is the Mother of God. Christ is God, who has become man.
Mix. 348-49

It (the doctrine of the Immaculate Conception of the Blessed Virgin) does but affirm that, together with the nature which she inherited from her parents, that is, her own nature, she had a superadded fullness of grace, and that from the first moment of her existence. Suppose Eve had stood the trial and not lost her first grace ... (her children) would have then been conceived in grace ... Mary may be called as it were a daughter of Eve unfallen ... to her the grace of God came ... from the first moment of her being, as it had been given to Eve.

Mary had the inward gift of grace from the first moment of her existence. Diff. II, 47

I consider it impossible then, for those who believe the Church to be one vast body in heaven and on earth, in which every holy creature of God has his place, and of which prayer is the life, when once they recognise the sanctity and the dignity of the Blessed Virgin, not to perceive immediately, that her office above is one of perpetual intercession for the faithful militant, and that our very relation to her must be that of clients to a patron, and that, in the eternal enmity which exists between the woman and the serpent, while the serpent's strength lies in being the tempter, the weapon of the second Eve and Mother of God is prayer.

Pray for us sinners now and at the hour of our death. Diff. II, 73

18. Life in the World and Love for Others

It would be a great mistake for us to suppose that we need quit our temporal calling, and go into retirement, in order to serve God acceptably. Christianity is a religion for the world, for the busy and influential, as well as for the poor.

Cardinal Newman spent his life preaching the Christian ideal to ordinary lay men and women. H.S. II, 94

The Christian will feel that the true contemplation of his Saviour lies in his worldly business; that as Christ is seen in the poor, and in the persecuted, and in children, so is he seen in the employments which he puts upon his chosen, whatever they be; that in attending to his own calling he will meet Christ; that if he neglect it, he will not on that account enjoy his presence at all the more, but that while performing it, he will see Christ revealed to his soul amid the ordinary actions of the day, as by a sort of sacrament.

This is 'the sacrament of the present moment'. P.S. VIII, 165

The works of each day, these are the tests of our glorious contemplations, whether or not they shall be available to our salvation; and he who does one deed of obedience for Christ's sake, let him have no imagination and no fine feeling, is a better man, and returns to his home justified rather than the most eloquent speaker.

By their fruits you shall know them. P.S. I, 270

We are to begin with loving our friends about us, and gradually to enlarge the circle of our affections, till it reaches all Christians, and then all men ... We see then how absurd it is, when writers ... talk magnificently about loving the whole human race with a comprehensive affection, of being friends of all mankind ... this is not to love men, it is but to talk of love. The real love of man must depend on practice.

That a thing is true is no reason that it should he said,
but that it should be done. P.S. II, 54–55

19. The Two Cities

How shall we persuade ourselves of the great truth that, in spite of outward appearances, human society, as we find it, is but part of an invisible world, and is really divided into two companies, the sons of God, and the children of the wicked one; that some souls are ministered unto by angels, others led captive by devils.

This is the Catholic doctrine of the warfare between the City of God and the powers of darkness. P.S. IV, 91

I prefer to live in an age when the fight is in the day, not in the twilight; and think it a gain to be speared by a foe, rather than to be stabbed by a friend … I hold that unbelief is in some shape unavoidable in an age of intellect and in a world like this, considering that faith requires an act of the will … It is one great advantage of an age in which unbelief speaks out, that faith can speak out too; that, if falsehood assails truth, truth can assail falsehood.

The advantage of living in a pluralistic world. Idea. 382

Time is short, eternity is long. Put not from you what you have here found: regard it not as mere matter of present controversy; set not out resolved to refute it, and looking about for the best way of doing so; seduce not yourself with the imagination that comes of disappointment, disgust, or restlessness, or wounded feeling, or undue sensibility, or other weakness. Wrap not yourself round in the associations of past years, nor determine that to be truth which you wish to be so, nor make an idol of cherished anticipations. Time is short, eternity is long.

These are the last words of The Development of Doctrine,
written as Cardinal Newman entered what he called
"the one fold of the redeemer". Dev. 445

20. The Last Things

O my Lord and Saviour, support me in that hour in the strong arms of thy Sacraments, and by the fresh fragrance of thy consolations. Let the absolving words be said over me, and the holy oil sign and seal me, and thy own Body be my food, and thy Blood my sprinkling; and let my sweet mother Mary breathe on me, and my angel whisper peace to me, and my glorious saints, and my own dear father, Philip, smile on me; that in them all, and through them all, I may receive the gift of perseverance, and die, as I desire to live, in thy faith, in thy Church, in thy service, and in thy love.

The Catholic's Prayer. Mix. 123

Eternity, or endlessness, is in itself mainly a negative idea, though the idea of suffering is positive. Its fearful force, as an element of future punishment, lies in what it excludes, it means never any change of state, no annihilation or restoration; but what, considered positively it adds to suffering, we do not know. For what we know, the suffering of one moment may in itself have no bearing, or but a partial bearing, on the suffering of the next; and thus, as far as its intensity is concerned, it may vary with every lost soul. This may be so, unless we assume that the suffering is necessarily attended by a consciousness of duration and succession.

We may try to make this part of the gospel less terrible to the imagination. G.A. 422

The Catholic Church allows no image of any sort, material or immaterial, no dogmatic symbol, no rite, no sacrament, no saint, not even the Blessed Virgin herself, to come between the soul and its Creator. It is face to face, "solus cum solo", in all matters between man and his God. He alone creates; he alone has redeemed; before his awful eyes we go in death; in the vision of him is our eternal beatitude.

Each one is made for union with God. Apo. 195

Reflections and Meditations

TO THE END OF THE LONGEST LIFE
YOU ARE STILL A BEGINNER.

(*Parochial and Plain Sermons*)

Our Christian Vocation

My vocation in life

God has created me to do him some definite service; he has committed some work to me which he has not committed to another. I have my mission – I never may know it in this life, but I shall be told it in the next. Somehow I am necessary for his purposes, as necessary in my place as an archangel in his – if, indeed, I fail, he can raise another as he could make the stones children of Abraham. Yet I have a part in this great work; I am a link in a chain, a bond of connection between persons. He has not created me for naught. I shall do good, I shall do his work; I shall be an angel of peace, a preacher of truth in my own place, while not intending it, if I do but keep his commandments and serve him in my calling. (Med.)

Complete trust in God's ways

Therefore I will trust him. Whatever, wherever I am, I can never be thrown away. If I am in sickness, my sickness may serve him; in perplexity, my perplexity may serve him; if I am in sorrow, my sorrow may serve him ... He does nothing in vain; he may prolong my life, he may shorten it; he knows what he is about. He may take away my friends, he may throw me among strangers, he may make me feel desolate, make my spirits sink, hide the future from me – still he knows what he is about. (Med.)

Submit to the loving will of God

Be sure that many others besides you feel that sadness, that years pass away and no opening comes to them for serving God ... One must submit oneself to God's loving will – and be quieted by faith that what he wills for us is best. He has no need of us – he only asks for our good desires. (Letter, October 1873)

It is God who leads us

We cannot have everything in this world but we can have the greatest of all, God's presence, God's guidance. May you have it abundantly, wherever you are, and you will, but you must leave yourself in his hands who loves you. (Letter, April 1853)

God knows what is best for us

Let us put ourselves into his hands, and not be startled though he leads us by a strange way, a *mirabilis via*, as the Church speaks. Let us be sure he will lead us right, that he will bring us to that which is not indeed what we think best, nor what is best for another, but what is best for us. (Med.)

Having the faith of Abraham

Abraham seems to have had something very noble and magnanimous about him. He could realise and make present to him things unseen. He followed God in the dark as promptly, as firmly, with as cheerful a heart, and bold a stepping, as if he were in broad daylight. There is something very great in this; and, therefore, St Paul calls Abraham our father, the father of Christians as well as Jews. For we are especially bound to walk by faith, not by sight; and are blessed in faith, and justified by faith, as was faithful Abraham. (P.S.)

How can I become perfect?

In a higher world it is otherwise, but here below to live is to change, and to be perfect is to have changed often. (Dev.)

Never standing still

If Christianity be an universal religion, suited not simply to one locality or period, but to all times and places, it cannot but vary in its relations and dealings towards the world around it, that is, it will develop. (Dev.)

God alone is constant

Life passes, riches fly away, popularity is fickle, the senses decay, the world changes, friends die. One alone is constant; one alone is true to us; one alone can be true; one alone can be all things to us. (P.S.)

A faithful God who never changes

All below heaven changes; spring, summer, autumn, each has its turn. The fortunes of the world change; what was high, lies low; what was low, rises high. Riches take wing and flee away; bereavements happen. Friends become enemies and enemies friends. Our wishes, aims and plans change. There is nothing stable but thou, O my God! And thou art the centre and life of all who change, who trust thee as their Father, who look to thee, and who are content to put themselves into thy hands. (Med.)

Only faith endures in changing times

Opinions change, conclusions are feeble, enquiries run their course, reason stops short, but faith alone reaches to the end, faith only endures. (Mix.)

Be Faithful in Little Things

Little acts of love

One little deed, done against natural inclination for God's sake, though in itself of a conceding or passive character, to brook an insult, to face a danger, or to resign an advantage, has in it a power outbalancing all the dust and chaff of mere profession. (U.S.)

Actions speak louder than words

Beware lest your religion be one of feeling merely, not of practice ... Many a man likes to be religious in graceful language; he loves religious tales and hymns, yet is never the better Christian for all this. The works of everyday, these are the tests of our glorious contemplations, whether or not they shall be available to our salvation; and he who does one deed of obedience for Christ's sake, let him have no imagination and no fine feeling, is a better man, and returns to his home justified rather than the most eloquent speaker and the most sensitive hearer, if such men do not practise up to their knowledge. (P.S.)

Does what you believe make a difference?

I really fear that most men called Christians, whatever they may profess, whatever they may think they feel, whatever warmth and illumination and love they may claim as their own, yet would go on almost as they do, neither much better nor much worse, if they believed Christianity to be a fable. (P.S.)

The sure road to perfection

It is the saying of holy men that, if we wish to be perfect, we have nothing more to do than to perform the ordinary duties of the day well. A short road to perfection – short, not because easy, but because pertinent and intelligible. There are no short ways to perfection, but there are sure ones. I think this is an instruction which may be of great practical use to persons like ourselves. It is easy to have vague ideas what perfection is, which serve well enough to talk about, when we do not intend to aim at it; but as soon as a person really desires and sets about seeking it himself he is dissatisfied with anything but what is tangible and clear, and constitutes some sort of direction towards the practice of it. (Med.)

Know your weakness

We must bear in mind what is meant by perfection. It does not mean any extraordinary service, anything out of the way, or especially heroic – not all have the opportunity of heroic acts, of sufferings – but it means what the word perfection ordinarily means. By perfect we mean that which has no flaw in it, that which is complete, that which is consistent, that which is sound – we mean the opposite to imperfect. As we know well what imperfection in religious service means, we know by the contrast what is meant by perfection. (Med.)

Perfect love in the ordinary things

He, then, is perfect who does the work of the day perfectly, and we need not go beyond this to seek for perfection. You need not go out of the round of the day. (Med.)

Ordinary daily mortification

I would not have you go to any mortifications. I will tell you what the greatest mortification is: to do well the ordinary duties of the day. Determine to rise at a certain hour – to go through certain devotions...

Don't oppress yourself with them, but keep to your rules – and you will find it a sufficient trial. (Letter, December 1850)

Living in the World

You cannot serve God and money

A smooth and easy life, an uninterrupted enjoyment of the goods of providence, full meals, soft raiment, well-furnished homes, the pleasures of sense, the feeling of security, the consciousness of wealth – these and the like, if we are not careful, choke up all the avenues of the soul through which the light and breath of heaven might come to us. (P.S.)

Assess the world with the eyes of faith

There are ten thousand ways of looking at this world, but only one right way. The man of pleasure has his way, the man of gain his, and the man of intellect his. Poor men and rich men, governors and governed, prosperous and discontented, learned and unlearned, each has his own way of looking at the things which come before him, and each has a wrong way. There is but one right way; it is the way in which God looks at the world. Aim at looking at it in God's way. Aim at seeing things as God sees them. Aim at forming judgements about persons, events, ranks, fortunes, changes, objects, such as God forms. Aim at looking at this life as God looks at it. Aim at looking at the life to come, and the world unseen as God does. Aim at seeing the king in his beauty. All things that we see are but shadows to us, and delusions, unless we enter into what they really mean. (P.S.)

Christ came to make a new world

He came into the world to regenerate it in himself, to make a new beginning, to be the beginning of the creation of God, to gather together in one, and recapitulate all things in himself. The rays of his glory were scattered through the world; one state of life had some of them, another others. The world was like some fair mirror, broken in pieces, and giving back no one uniform image of its Maker. But he came to combine what was dissipated, to recast what was shattered in himself. He began all excellence, and of his fullness have we all received. (S.D.)

How to use our intellect

I say that a cultivated intellect, because it is a good in itself, brings with it a power and a grace to every work and occupation which it undertakes, and enables us to be more useful, and to a greater number. There is a duty we owe to human society as such, to the state to which we belong, to the sphere in which we move. (Idea)

Duties and role of a layperson

I want an intelligent, well-instructed laity. I wish you to enlarge your knowledge, to cultivate your reason, to understand how faith and reason stand to each other, what are the bases and principles of Catholicism. (Prepos.)

Treat knowledge carefully

Knowledge, viewed as knowledge, exerts a subtle influence in throwing us back on ourselves, and making us our own centre, and our own minds the measure of all things. (Idea)

Young people facing the world about them

We have most of us by nature longings more or less, and aspirations, after something greater than this world can give. Youth, especially has a natural love of what is noble and heroic. We like to hear marvellous tales, which throw us out of things as they are, and introduce us to things that are not. We so love the idea of the invisible that we even build fabrics in the air for ourselves, if heavenly truth be not vouchsafed us. We love to fancy ourselves involved in circumstances of danger or trial, and acquitting ourselves well under them. Or we imagine some perfection, such as earth has not, which we follow, and render it our homage and our heart. Such is the state more or less of young persons before the world alters them, before the world comes upon them, as it often does very soon, with its polluting, withering, debasing, deadening influence, before it breathes on them, and blights and parches, and strips off their green foliage, and leaves there, as dry and wintry trees without sap or sweetness. But in early youth we stand with our leaves and blossoms on which promise fruit; we stand by the side of the still waters, with our hearts beating high, with longings after our unknown good, and with a sort of contempt for the fashions of the world; with a contempt for the world, even though we engage in it... (P.S.)

Developing my Faith

True discernment

Beware of trifling with your conscience. It is often said that second thoughts are best; so they are in matters of judgement, but not in matters of conscience. In matters of duty first thoughts are commonly best – they have more in them of the voice of God. (P.S.)

Developing your conscience

Certainly I have always contended that obedience, even to an erring conscience was the way to gain light, and that it mattered not where a man began, so that he began on what came to hand, and in faith; and that any thing might become a divine method of truth; that to the pure all things are pure, and have a self-correcting virtue and a power of germinating. (Apo.)

Role of my intellect and my faith

You must not suppose that I am denying the intellect its real place in the discovery of truth, but it must ever be borne in mind that its exercise mainly consists of reasoning – that is, in comparing things, classifying them, and inferring. It ever needs points to start from, first principles, and these it does not provide – but it can no more move one step without these starting points, than a stick, which supports a man, can move without the man's action ... To gain religious starting points, we must interrogate our hearts, and (since it is a personal, individual matter) our own hearts – interrogate our own consciences, interrogate, I will say, the God who dwells there. (Letter, June 1869)

Grounds for being a Catholic

I am a Catholic by virtue of my believing in a God; and if I am asked why I believe in a God, I answer that it is because I believe in myself, for I feel it impossible to believe in my own existence (and of that fact I am quite sure) without believing also in the existence of him, who lives as a personal, all-seeing, all-judging being in my conscience. (Apo.)

Human love inspired by divine love

We find our Saviour had a private friend; and this shows us, first, how entirely he was a man, as much as any of us, in his wants and feelings; and next, that there is nothing contrary to the spirit of the Gospel, nothing inconsistent with the fullness of Christian love, in having our affections directed in an especial way towards certain objects, towards those whom the circumstances of our past life, or some peculiarities of character, have endeared to us. (P.S.)

Living as a True Witness

Our prayers open heaven to the world

Let us but raise the level of religion in our hearts and it will rise in the world. He who attempts to set up God's Kingdom in his heart, furthers it in the world. He whose prayers come up for a memorial before God, opens the windows of heaven, and the foundations of the great deep, and the waters rise. (P.S.)

How can I be a witness to Christ?

Stay with me, and then I shall begin to shine as thou shinest: so to shine as to be a light to others. The light, O Jesus, will be all from thee. None of it will be mine. No merit to me. It will be thou who shinest through me upon others. O let me thus praise thee, in the way which thou dost love best, by shining on all those around me. Give light to them as well as to me; light them with me, through me. Teach me to show forth thy praise, thy truth, thy will. Make me preach thee without preaching – not by words, but by my example and by the catching force, the sympathetic

113

influence, of what I do – by my visible resemblance to thy saints, and the evident fullness of the love which my heart bears to thee. (Med.)

Preaching the good news

Christianity is eminently an objective religion. For the most part it tells us of persons and facts in simple words, and leaves that announcement to produce its effect on such hearts as are prepared to receive it. (Dev.)

How can I speak about my religion?

What I have been saying comes to this – be in earnest, and you will speak of religion where, and when, and how you should; aim at things, and your words will be right without aiming. (P.S.)

The Holy Spirit is my defender

No one, doubtless, can deny this most gracious and consolatory truth that the Holy Ghost is come; but why has he come? To supply Christ's absence, or to accomplish his presence? Surely to make him present. Let us not for a moment suppose that God the Holy Ghost comes in such sense that God the Son remains away. No, he has not so come that Christ does not come, but rather he comes that Christ may come in his coming. Through the Holy Ghost we have communion with the Father and the Son. (P.S.)

Christ's love for the lonely

Let all those who are in trouble take this comfort to themselves, if they are trying to lead a spiritual life. If they call on God, he will answer them. Though they have no earthly friend, they have him, who, as he felt for his mother when he was on the cross, now that he is in his glory, feels for the lowest and feeblest of his people. (Med.)

Come Holy Spirit, come to me

Thou alone canst fill the soul of man, and thou hast promised to do so. Thou art the living flame, and ever burnest with love of man: enter into me and set me on fire after thy pattern and likeness. (Med.)

Mary is my mother

Mary is exalted for the sake of Jesus. It was fitting that she, as being a creature, though the first of creatures, should have an office of ministration. She, as others, came into the world to do a work, she had a mission to fulfil; her grace and her glory are not for her own sake but for her Maker's; and to her is committed the custody of the Incarnation ... her glories and the devotion paid her proclaim and define the right faith concerning him as God and man. (Mix.)

True Christian Wisdom

The wisdom that comes with age

As time goes on you will know yourself better and better. Time does that for us, not only by the increase of experience, but by the withdrawal of those natural assistances to devotion and self-surrender which youth furnishes. When the spirits are high and the mind fervent, though we may have waywardness and perverseness which we have not afterwards, yet we have something to battle against them. But when men get old ... then they see how little grace is in them, and how much what seemed grace was but nature. (Letter, July 1850)

Accepting our true poverty

With old age the soul is left to lassitude, torpor, dejection and coldness which is its real state, with no natural impulses, affections or imaginations to rouse it and things which in youth seemed easy then become difficult. Then it finds how little self-command it has, and how little it can throw off the tempter when he comes behind and places it in a certain direction or position, or throws it down, or places his foot upon it. Then it understands at length its own nothingness, and that it has less grace than it had but it has nothing but grace to aid it. It is the sign of a saint to grow; common minds, even though they are in the grace of God, dwindle, (i.e. seem to do so) as time goes on. (Letter, July 1850)

In old age turn to Mary

The energy of grace alone can make a soul strong in age. Do not then be cast down, if you though not very aged feel less fervent than you did ten years since – only let it be a call on you to seek grace to supply nature, as well as to overcome it. Put yourself ever fully and utterly into Mary's hands and she will nurse you and bring you forward. She will watch over you as a mother over a sick child. (Letter, July 1850)

Time passes relentlessly on

There is something awful in the silent resistless sweep of time – and, as years go on, and friends are taken away, one draws the thought of those who remain about one, as in cold weather one buttons up great coats and capes, for protection. (Letter, January 1860)

Perfection through obedience to God

Pray him to give you what Scripture calls "an honest or good heart", or a "perfect heart", and, without waiting, begin at once to obey him with the best heart you have. Any obedience is better than none – any profession which is disjoined from obedience, is a mere pretence and deceit. Any religion which does not bring you nearer to God is of the world. You have to seek his face; obedience is the only way of seeking him. All your duties are obediences. If you are to believe the truths he has revealed, to regulate yourselves by his precepts, to be frequent in his ordinances, to adhere to his Church and people, why is it, except because he has bid you? And to do what he bids is to obey him, and to obey him is to approach him. (P.S.)

Life is short and death is certain

Every act of obedience is an approach – an approach to him who is not far off, though he seems so, but close behind this visible screen of things which hides him from us. He is behind this material framework; earth and sky are but a veil going between him and us; the day will come when he will rend that veil, and show himself to us. And then, according as we have waited for him, will he recompense us. If we have forgotten him, he will not know us, but

> blessed are those servants whom the Lord, when he cometh, shall find watching... he shall gird himself, and make them sit down to meat, and will come forth and serve them. And if he shall come in the second watch, or come in the third watch, and find them so, blessed are those servants.

May this be the portion of every one of us! It is hard to attain it; but it is woeful to fail. Life is short; death is certain; and the world to come is everlasting. (P.S.)

What do I think about dying?

Looking beyond this life, my first prayer, aim and hope is that I may see God. The thought of being blest with the sight of earthly friends pales before that thought. I believe that I shall never die; this awful prospect would crush me, were it not that I trusted and prayed that it would be an eternity in God's presence. How is eternity a boon unless he goes with it? And for others dear to me, my one prayer is that they may see God. (Letter, February 1880)

Peace at the last

May he support us all the day long, till the shades lengthen, and the evening comes, and the busy world is hushed, and the fever of life is over, and our work is done. Then in his mercy may he give us a safe lodging, and a holy rest, and peace at the last. (S.D.)

Hymns and Prayers

PRAISE TO THE HOLIEST
IN THE HEIGHT

Praise to the holiest in the height;
　　And in the depth be praise:
In all his words most wonderful;
Most sure in all his ways.

O loving wisdom of our God!
When all was sin and shame,
A second Adam to the fight
And to the rescue came.

O wisest love! That flesh and blood
Which did in Adam fail,
Should strive afresh against the foe,
Should strive and should prevail.

And that a higher gift than grace
Should flesh and blood refine,
God's presence and his very self,
And essence all divine.

O generous love! That he who smote
In man for man the foe,
The double agony in man
For man should undergo.

And in the garden secretly
And on the cross on high,
Should teach his brethren and inspire
To suffer and to die.

ANIMA CHRISTI

Soul of Christ, be my sanctification;
Body of Christ, be my salvation;
Blood of Christ, fill all my veins;
Water of Christ's side, wash out my stains;
Passion of Christ, my comfort be;
O good Jesu, listen to me;
In thy wounds I fain would hide,
Ne'er to be parted from thy side;
Guard me, should the foe assail me;
Call me when my life shall fail me,
Bid me come to thee above,
With thy saints to sing thy love,
World without end. Amen.

LEAD KINDLY LIGHT

Lead, kindly light, amid the encircling gloom,
Lead thou me on!
The night is dark, and I am far from home, –
Lead thou me on!
Keep thou my feet; I do not ask to see
The distant scene, – one step enough for me.

It was not ever thus, nor pray'd that thou
Shouldst lead me on.
I loved to choose and see my path, but now
Lead thou me on!
I loved the garish day, and spite of fears,
Pride ruled my will: remember not past years.

So long thy power hath blest me, sure it still
Will lead me on,
O'er moor and fen, o'er crag and torrent, till
The night is gone;
And with the morn those angel faces smile
Which I have lov'd long since, and lost awhile.

THE LAST THINGS

Jesu, Maria – I am near to death,
    And thou art calling me; I know it now,
  Not by the token of this faltering breath,
This chill at heart, this dampness on my brow, –
(Jesu, have mercy! Mary, pray for me!)
'Tis this new feeling, never felt before,
(Be with me, Lord, in my extremity!)
That I am going, that I am no more,
'Tis this strange innermost abandonment
(Lover of souls! Great God! I look to thee,)
This emptying out of each constituent
And natural force, by which I come to be.
Pray for me, O my friends; a visitant
Is knocking his dire summons at my door,
The like of whom, to scare me and to daunt,
Has never, never come to me before.

(from *The Dream of Gerontius*)

RAISED FROM THE DEAD

Take me away, and in the lowest deep
   There let me be,
And there in hope the lone night-watches keep,
Told out for me.
There, motionless and happy in my pain,
Lone, not forlorn, –
There will I sing my sad perpetual strain,
Until the morn.
There will I sing, and soothe my stricken breast,
Which ne'er can cease
To throb, and pine, and languish, till possest
Of its sole peace.
There will I sing my absent Lord and Love: –
Take me away
That sooner I may rise, and go above,
And see him in the truth of everlasting day.

(from *The Dream of Gerontius*)

PART III

THREE SERMONS
BY JOHN HENRY NEWMAN

The Second Spring

Preached on 13th July, 1852, in St Mary's College, Oscott, in the First Provincial Synod of Westminster, before Cardinal Wiseman and the Bishops of England. First published in *Sermons Preached on Various Occasions.*

Surge, propera, amica mea, columba mea, formosa mea, et veni. Jam enim hiems transiit, imber abiit et recessit. Flores apparuerunt in terra nostra. CANT., c. ii. v. 10–12.

Arise, make haste, my love, my dove, my beautiful one, and come. For the winter is now past, the rain is over and gone. The flowers have appeared in our land.

We have familiar experience of the order, the constancy, the perpetual renovation of the material world which surrounds us. Frail and transitory as is every part of it, restless and migratory as are its elements, never-ceasing as are its changes, still it abides. It is bound together by a law of permanence, it is set up in unity; and, though it is ever dying, it is ever coming to life again. Dissolution does but give birth to fresh modes of organisation, and one death is the parent of a thousand lives. Each hour, as it comes, is but a testimony, how fleeting, yet how secure, how certain, is the great whole. It is like an image on the waters, which is ever the same, though the waters ever flow. Change upon change, yet one change cries out to another, like the alternate Seraphim, in praise and in glory of their Maker. The sun sinks to rise again; the day is swallowed up in the gloom of the night, to be born out of it, as fresh as if it had never been quenched. Spring passes into summer, and through summer and autumn into winter, only the more surely, by its own ultimate return, to triumph over that grave, towards which it resolutely hastened from its first hour. We mourn over the blossoms of May, because they are to wither; but we know, withal, that May is one day to have its revenge upon November, by the revolution of that solemn circle which never stops, which teaches us in our height of hope, ever to be sober, and in our depth of desolation, never to despair.

And forcibly as this comes home to every one of us, not less forcible is the contrast which exists between this material world, so vigorous, so reproductive, amid all its changes, and the moral world, so feeble, so downward, so resourceless, amid all its aspirations. That which ought to come to nought, endures; that which promises a future, disappoints and is no more. The same sun shines in heaven from first to last, and the blue firmament, the everlasting mountains, reflect his rays; but where is there upon earth the champion, the hero, the lawgiver, the body politic, the sovereign race, which was great three hundred years ago, and is great now? Moralists and poets, often do they descant upon this innate vitality of matter, this innate perishableness of mind. Man rises to fall: he tends to dissolution from the moment he begins to be; he lives on, indeed, in his children, he lives on in his name, he lives not on in his own person. He is, as regards the manifestations of his nature here below, as a bubble that breaks, and as water poured out upon the earth. He was young, he is old, he is never young again. This is the lament over him, poured forth in verse and in prose, by Christians and by heathen. The greatest work of God's hands under the sun, he, in all the manifestations of his complex being, is born only to die.

His bodily frame first begins to feel the power of this constraining law, though it is the last to succumb to it. We look at the bloom of youth with interest, yet with pity; and the more graceful and sweet it is, with pity so much the more; for, whatever be its excellence and its glory, soon it begins to be deformed and dishonoured by the very force of its living on. It grows into exhaustion and collapse, till at length it crumbles into that dust out of which it was originally taken.

So is it, too, with our moral being, a far higher and diviner portion of our natural constitution; it begins with life, it ends with what is worse than the mere loss of life, with a living death. How beautiful is the human heart, when it puts forth its first leaves, and opens and rejoices in its spring-tide. Fair as may be the bodily form, fairer far, in its green foliage and bright blossoms, its natural virtue. It blooms in the young, like some rich flower, so delicate, so fragrant, and so dazzling. Generosity and lightness of heart and amiableness, the confiding spirit, the gentle temper, the elastic cheerfulness, the open hand, the pure affection, the noble aspiration, the heroic resolve, the romantic pursuit, the love in which self has no part, are not these beautiful? And are they not dressed up and set forth for admiration in their best shapes, in tales and in poems? And ah! What a prospect of good is there! Who could believe that it is to fade! And yet, as night follows upon day, as decrepitude follows upon health, so surely are failure, and overthrow, and annihilation, the issue of this natural virtue, if time only be allowed to it to run its course. There are those who are cut off in the first opening of this excellence, and then, if we may trust their epitaphs, they have lived like angels; but wait a while, let them live on, let the course of life proceed, let the bright soul go through the fire and water of the world's temptations and seductions and corruptions and transformations; and, alas for the insufficiency of nature! Alas for its powerlessness to persevere, its waywardness in disappointing its own promise! Wait till youth has become age; and not more different is the miniature which we have of him when a boy, when every feature spoke of hope, put side by side of the large portrait painted to his honour, when he is old, when his limbs are shrunk, his eye dim, his brow furrowed, and his hair grey, than differs the moral grace of that boyhood from the forbidding and repulsive aspect of his soul, now that he has lived to the age of man. For moroseness, and misanthropy, and selfishness, is the ordinary winter of that spring.

Such is man in his own nature, and such, too, is he in his works. The noblest efforts of his genius, the conquests he has made, the doctrines he has originated, the nations he has civilised, the states he has created, they outlive himself, they outlive him by many centuries, but they tend to an end, and that end is dissolution. Powers of the world, sovereignties, dynasties, sooner or later come to nought; they have their fatal hour. The Roman conqueror shed tears over Carthage, for in the destruction of the rival city he discerned too truly an augury of the fall of Rome; and at length, with the weight and the responsibilities, the crimes and the glories, of centuries upon centuries, the Imperial City fell.

Thus man and all his works are mortal; they die, and they have no power of renovation.

But what is it, my Fathers, my Brothers, what is it that has happened in England just at this time? Something strange is passing over this land, by the very surprise, by the very commotion, which it excites. Were we not near enough the scene of action to be able to say what is going on, were we the inhabitants of some sister planet possessed of a more perfect mechanism than this earth has discovered for surveying the transactions of another globe, and did we turn our eyes thence towards England just at this season, we should be arrested by a political phenomenon as wonderful as any which the astronomer notes down from his physical field of view. It would be the occurrence of a national commotion, almost without parallel, more violent than has happened here for centuries, at least in the judgements and intentions of men, if not in act and deed. We should note it down, that soon after St Michael's day, 1850, a storm arose in the moral world, so furious as to demand some great explanation, and to rouse in us an intense desire to gain it. We should observe it increasing from day to day, and spreading from place to place, without remission, almost without lull, up to this very hour, when perhaps it threatens worse still, or at least gives no sure prospect of alleviation. Every party in the body politic undergoes its influence, from the Queen upon her throne, down to the little ones in the infant or day school. The ten thousands of the constituency, the sum total of Protestant sects, the aggregate of religious societies and associations, the great body of established clergy in town and country, the bar, even the medical profession, nay, even literary and scientific circles, every class, every interest, every fireside, gives tokens of this ubiquitous storm. This would be our report of it, seeing it from the distance, and we should speculate on the cause. What is it all about? Against what is it directed? What wonder has happened upon earth? What prodigious, what preternatural event is adequate to the burden of so vast an effect?

We should judge rightly in our curiosity about a phenomenon like this; it must be a portentous event, and it is. It is an innovation, a miracle, I may say, in the course of human events. The physical world revolves year by year, and begins again; but the political order of things does not renew itself, does not return; it continues, but it proceeds; there is no retrogression. This is so well understood by men of the day, that with them progress is idolised as another name for good. The past never returns – it is never good; if we are to escape existing ills, it must be by going forward. The past is out of date; the past is dead. As well may the dead live to us, as well may the dead profit us, as the past return. This, then, is the cause of this national transport, this national cry, which encompasses us. The past has returned, the dead lives. Thrones are overturned, and are never restored; States live and die, and then are matter only for history. Babylon was great, and Tyre, and Egypt, and Nineve, and shall never be great again. The English Church was, and the English Church was not, and the English Church is once again. This is the portent, worthy of a cry. It is the coming in of a Second Spring; it is a restoration in the moral world, such as that which yearly takes place in the physical.

Three centuries ago, and the Catholic Church, that great creation of God's power, stood in this land in pride of place. It had the honours of near a thousand years upon it; it was enthroned in some twenty sees up and down the broad country; it was based in the will of a faithful people; it energised through ten thousand instruments of power and influence; and it was ennobled by a host of saints and martyrs. The churches, one by one, recounted and rejoiced in the line of glorified intercessors, who were the respective objects of their grateful homage. Canterbury alone numbered perhaps some sixteen, from St Augustine to St Dunstan and St Elphege, from St Anselm and St Thomas down to St Edmund.

York had its St Paulinus, St John, St Wilfrid, and St William; London, its St Erconwald; Durham, its St Cuthbert; Winton, its St Swithun. Then there were St Aidan of Lindisfarne, and St Hugh of Lincoln, and

St Chad of Lichfield, and St Thomas of Hereford, and St Oswald and St Wulstan of Worcester, and St Osmund of Salisbury, and St Birinus of Dorchester, and St Richard of Chichester. And then, too, its religious orders, its monastic establishments, its universities, its wide relations all over Europe, its high prerogatives in the temporal state, its wealth, its dependencies, its popular honours, where was there in the whole of Christendom a more glorious hierarchy? Mixed up with the civil institutions, with king and nobles, with the people, found in every village and in every town, it seemed destined to stand, so long as England stood, and to outlast, it might be, England's greatness.

But it was the high decree of heaven, that the majesty of that presence should be blotted out. It is a long story, my Fathers and Brothers – you know it well. I need not go through it. The vivifying principle of truth, the shadow of St Peter, the grace of the Redeemer, left it. That old Church in its day became a corpse (a marvellous, an awful change!); and then it did but corrupt the air which once it refreshed, and cumber the ground which once it beautified. So all seemed to be lost; and there was a struggle for a time, and then its priests were cast out or martyred. There were sacrileges innumerable. Its temples were profaned or destroyed; its revenues seized by covetous nobles, or squandered upon the ministers of a new faith. The presence of Catholicism was at length simply removed, its grace disowned, its power despised, its name, except as a matter of history, at length almost unknown. It took a long time to do this thoroughly; much time, much thought, much labour, much expense; but at last it was done.

Oh, that miserable day, centuries before we were born! What a martyrdom to live in it and see the fair form of truth, moral and material, hacked piecemeal, and every limb and organ carried off, and burned in the fire, or cast into the deep! But at last the work was done. Truth was disposed of, and shovelled away, and there was a calm, a silence, a sort of peace; and such was about the state of things when we were born into this weary world.

My Fathers and Brothers, you have seen it on one side, and some of us on another; but one and all of us can bear witness to the fact of the utter contempt into which Catholicism had fallen by the time that we were born. You, alas, know it far better than I can know it; but it may not be out of place, if by one or two tokens, as by the strokes of a pencil, I bear witness to you from without, of what you can witness so much more truly from within. No longer, the Catholic Church in the country; nay, no longer I may say, a Catholic community; but a few adherents of the Old Religion, moving silently and sorrowfully about, as memorials of what had been. "The Roman Catholics;" not a sect, not even an interest, as men conceived of it, not a body, however small, representative of the Great Communion abroad, but a mere handful of individuals, who might be counted, like the pebbles and detritus of the great deluge, and who, forsooth, merely happened to retain a creed which, in its day indeed, was the profession of a Church. Here a set of poor Irishmen, coming and going at harvest time, or a colony of them lodged in a miserable quarter of the vast metropolis. There, perhaps an elderly person, seen walking in the streets, grave and solitary, and strange, though noble in bearing, and said to be of good family, and a "Roman Catholic." An old-fashioned house of gloomy appearance, closed in with high walls, with an iron gate, and yews, and the report attaching to it that "Roman Catholics" lived there; but who they were, or what they did, or what was meant by calling them Roman Catholics, no one could tell; though it had an unpleasant sound, and told of form and superstition.

And then, perhaps, as we went to and fro, looking with a boy's curious eyes through the great city, we might come today upon some Moravian chapel, or Quaker's meeting-house, and tomorrow on a chapel of the "Roman Catholics" but nothing was to be gathered from it, except that there were lights burning there, and some boys in white, swinging censers; and what it all meant could only be learned from books, from Protestant histories and sermons; and they did not report well of "the Roman Catholics" but, on the contrary, deposed that they had once had power and had abused it. And then, again, we might, on one occasion, hear it pointedly put out by some literary man, as the result of his careful investigation, and as a recondite point of information, which few knew, that there was this difference between the Roman Catholics of England and the Roman Catholics of Ireland, that the latter had bishops, and the former were governed by four officials, called Vicars Apostolic.

Such was about the sort of knowledge possessed of Christianity by the heathen of old time, who persecuted its adherents from the face of the earth, and then called them a *gens lucifuga*, a people who shunned the light of day. Such were Catholics in England, found in corners, and alleys, and cellars, and the housetops, or in the recesses of the country; cut off from the populous world around them, and dimly seen, as if through a mist or in twilight, as ghosts flitting to and fro, by the high Protestants, the lords of the earth. At length so feeble did they become, so utterly contemptible, that contempt gave birth to pity; and the more generous of their tyrants actually began to wish to bestow on them some favour, under the notion that their opinions were simply too absurd ever to spread again, and that they themselves, were they but raised in civil importance, would soon unlearn and be ashamed of them. And thus, out of mere kindness to us, they began to vilify our doctrines to the Protestant world, that so our very idiocy or our secret unbelief might be our plea for mercy.

A great change, an awful contrast, between the time-honoured Church of St Augustine and St Thomas, and the poor remnant of their children in the beginning of the nineteenth century! It was a miracle, I might say, to have pulled down that lordly power; but there was a greater and a truer one in store. No one could have prophesied its fall, but still less would anyone have ventured to prophesy its rise again. The fall was wonderful; still after all it was in the order of nature; all things come to nought: its rise again would be a different sort of wonder, for it is in the order of grace, and who can hope for miracles, and such a miracle as this! Has the whole course of history a like to show? I must speak cautiously and according to my knowledge, but I recollect no parallel to it. Augustine, indeed, came to the same island to which the early missionaries had come already; but they came to Britons, and he to Saxons. The Arian Goths and Lombards, too, cast off their heresy in St Augustine's age, and joined the Church; but they had never fallen away from her. The inspired word seems to imply the almost impossibility of such a grace as the renovation of those who have crucified to themselves again, and trodden underfoot, the Son of God. Who then could have dared to hope that, out of so sacrilegious a nation as this is, a people would have been formed again unto their Saviour? What signs did it show that it was to be singled out from among the nations? Had it been prophesied some fifty years ago, would not the very notion have seemed preposterous and wild?

My Fathers, there was one of your own order, then in the maturity of his powers and his reputation. His name is the property of this diocese; yet is too great, too venerable, too dear to all Catholics, to be confined to any part of England, when it is rather a household word in the mouths of all of us. What would have been the feelings of that venerable man, the champion of God's ark in an evil time, could he have lived to see this day? It is almost presumptuous for one who knew him not, to draw pictures about him, and his thoughts, and his friends, some of whom are even here present;

yet am I wrong in fancying that a day such as this, in which we stand, would have seemed to him a dream, or, if he prophesied of it, to his hearers nothing but a mockery? Say that one time, rapt in spirit, he had reached forward to the future, and that his mortal eye had wandered from that lowly chapel in the valley which had been for centuries in the possession of Catholics, to the neighbouring height, then waste and solitary. And let him say to those about him: "I see a bleak mount, looking upon an open country, over against that huge town, to whose inhabitants Catholicism is of so little account. I see the ground marked out, and an ample enclosure made; and plantations are rising there, clothing and circling in the space."

And there on that high spot, far from the haunts of men, yet in the very centre of the island, a large edifice, or rather pile of edifices, appears, with many fronts and courts, and long cloisters and corridors, and story upon story. And there it rises, under the invocation of the same sweet and powerful name which has been our strength and consolation in the Valley. I look more attentively at that building, and I see it is fashioned upon that ancient style of art which brings back the past, which had seemed to be perishing from off the face of the earth, or to be preserved only as a curiosity, or to be imitated only as a fancy. I listen, and I hear the sound of voices, grave and musical, renewing the old chant, with which Augustine greeted Ethelbert in the free air upon the Kentish strand. It comes from a long procession, and it winds along the cloisters. Priests and Religious, theologians from the schools, and canons from the Cathedral, walk in due precedence. And then there comes a vision of well-nigh twelve mitred heads; and last I see a Prince of the Church, in the royal dye of empire and of martyrdom, a pledge to us from Rome of Rome's unwearied love, a token that that goodly company is firm in Apostolic faith and hope. And the shadow of the saints is there; St Benedict is there, speaking to us by the voice of bishop and of priest, and counting over the long ages through which he has prayed, and studied, and laboured; there, too, is St Dominic's white wool, which no blemish can impair, no stain can dim: and if St Bernard be not there, it is only that his absence may make him be remembered more. And the princely patriarch, St Ignatius, too, the St George of the modern world, with his chivalrous lance run through his writhing foe, he, too, sheds his blessing upon that train. And others, also, his equals or his juniors in history, whose pictures are above our altars, or soon shall be, the surest proof that the Lord's arm has not waxen short, nor his mercy failed, they, too, are looking down from their thrones on high upon the throng. And so that high company moves on into the holy place; and there, with august rite and awful sacrifice, inaugurates the great act which brings it thither.

What is that act? It is the first synod of a new Hierarchy; it is the resurrection of the Church.

O my Fathers, my Brothers, had that revered bishop spoken then, who that had heard him but would have said that he spoke what could not be? What! Those few scattered worshippers, the Roman Catholics, to form a Church! Shall the past be rolled back? Shall the grave open? Shall the Saxons live again to God? Shall the shepherds, watching their poor flocks by night, be visited by a multitude of the heavenly army, and hear how their Lord has been new-born in their own city? Yes; for grace can, where nature cannot. The world grows old, but the Church is ever young. She can, in any time, at her Lord's will, "inherit the Gentiles, and inhabit the desolate cities."

Arise, Jerusalem, for thy light is come, and the glory of the Lord is risen upon thee. Behold, darkness shall cover the earth, and a mist the people; but the Lord shall arise upon thee, and his glory shall be seen upon thee. Lift up thine eyes round about, and see; all these are gathered together, they come to thee; thy sons shall come from afar, and thy daughters shall rise up at thy side." "Arise, make haste, my love, my dove, my beautiful one, and come. For the winter is now past, and the rain is over and gone. The flowers have appeared in our land ... the fig-tree hath put forth her green figs; the vines in flower yield their sweet smell. Arise, my love, my beautiful one, and come.

It is the time for thy Visitation. Arise, Mary, and go forth in thy strength into that North Country, which once was thine own, and take possession of a land which knows thee not. Arise, Mother of God, and with thy thrilling voice, speak to those who labour with child, and are in pain, till the babe of grace leaps within them? Shine on us, dear Lady, with thy bright countenance, like the sun in his strength, O *stella matutina*, O harbinger of peace, till our year is one perpetual May. From thy sweet eyes, from thy pure smile, from thy majestic brow, let ten thousand influences rain down, not to confound or overwhelm, but to persuade, to win over thine enemies. O Mary, my hope, O Mother undefiled, fulfil to us the promise of this Spring. A second temple rises on the ruins of the old. Canterbury has gone its way, and York is gone, and Durham is gone, and Winchester is gone. It was sore to part with them. We clung to the vision of past greatness, and would not believe it could come to nought; but the Church in England has died, and the Church lives again. Westminster and Nottingham, Beverley and Hexham, Northampton and Shrewsbury, if the world lasts, shall be names as musical to the ear, as stirring to the heart, as the glories we have lost; and saints shall rise out of them, if God so will, and doctors once again shall give the law to Israel, and preachers call to penance and to justice, as at the beginning.

Yes, my Fathers and Brothers, and if it be God's blessed will, not saints alone, not doctors only, not preachers only, shall be ours, but martyrs, too, shall reconsecrate the soil to God. We know not what is before us, ere we win our own; we are engaged in a great, a joyful work, but in proportion to God's grace is the fury of his enemies. They have welcomed us as the lion greets his prey. Perhaps they may be familiarised in time with our appearance, but perhaps they may be irritated the more. To set up the Church again in England is too great an act to be done in a corner. We have had reason to expect that such a boon would not be given to us without a cross. It is not God's way that great blessings should descend without the sacrifice first of great sufferings. If the truth is to be spread to any wide extent among this people, how can we dream, how can we hope, that trial and trouble shall not accompany its going forth? And we have already, if it may be said without presumption, to commence our work withal, a large store of merits. We have no slight outfit for our opening warfare. Can we religiously suppose that the blood of our martyrs, three centuries ago and since, shall never receive its recompense? Those priests, secular and regular, did they suffer for no end? Or rather, for an end which is not yet accomplished? The long imprisonment, the fetid dungeon, the weary suspense, the tyrannous trial, the barbarous sentence, the savage execution, the rack, the gibbet, the knife, the cauldron, the numberless tortures of those holy victims, O my God, are they to have no reward? Are thy martyrs to cry from under thine altar for their loving vengeance on this guilty people, and to cry in vain? Shall they lose life, and not gain a better life for the children of those who persecuted them? Is this thy way, O my God, righteous and true? Is it according to thy promise, O king of saints, if I may dare talk to thee of justice? Did not thou thyself pray for thine enemies upon the cross, and convert them? Did not thy first martyr win thy great apostle, then a persecutor, by his loving prayer? And in that day of trial and desolation for England, when hearts were pierced through and through with Mary's woe, at the crucifixion of thy body mystical, was not every tear that flowed, and every drop of blood that was shed, the seeds of a future harvest, when they who sowed in sorrow were to reap in joy?

And as that suffering of the martyrs is not yet recompensed, so, perchance, it is not yet exhausted. Something for what we know, remains to be undergone, to complete the necessary sacrifice. May God forbid it, for this poor nation's sake! But still could we be surprised, my Fathers and my Brothers, if the winter even now should not yet be quite over? Have we any right to take it strange, if, in this English land, the spring-time of the Church should turn out to be an English spring, an uncertain, anxious time of hope and fear, of joy and suffering, of bright promise and budding hopes, yet withal, of keen blasts, and cold showers, and sudden storms?

One thing alone I know – that according to our need, so will be our strength. One thing I am sure of, that the more the enemy rages against us, so much the more will the saints in heaven plead for us; the more fearful are our trials from the world, the more present to us will be our Mother Mary, and our good patrons, and Angel Guardians; the more malicious are the devices of men against us, the louder cry of supplication will ascend from the bosom of the whole Church to God for us. We shall not be left orphans;

we shall have within us the strength of the Paraclete, promised to the Church and to every member of it. My Fathers, my Brothers in the priesthood, I speak from my heart when I declare my conviction, that there is no one among you here present but, if God so willed, would readily become a martyr for his sake. I do not say you would wish it; I do not say that – the natural will would not pray that that chalice might pass away; I do not speak of what you can do by any strength of yours; but in the strength of God, in the grace of the Spirit, in the armour of justice, by the consolations and peace of the Church, by the blessing of the apostles Peter and Paul, and in the name of Christ, you would do what nature cannot do. By the intercession of the saints on high, by the penances and good works and the prayers of the people of God on earth, you would be forcibly borne up as upon the waves of the mighty deep, and carried on out of yourselves by the fullness of grace, whether nature wished it or no. I do not mean violently, or with unseemly struggle, but calmly, gracefully, sweetly, joyously, you would mount up and ride forth to the battle, as on the rush of angel's wings, as your fathers did before you, and gained the prize. You, who day by day offer up the Immaculate Lamb of God, you who hold in your hands the Incarnate Word under the visible tokens which he has ordained, you who again and again drain the chalice of the Great Victim; who is to make you fear? What is to startle you? What to seduce you? Who is to stop you, whether you are to suffer or to do, whether to lay the foundations of the

Church in tears, or to put the crown upon the work in jubilation?

My Fathers, my Brothers, one word more. It may seem as if I were going out of my way in thus addressing you; but I have some sort of plea to urge in extenuation. When the English College at Rome was set up by the solicitude of a great Pontiff in the beginning of England's sorrows, and missionaries were trained there for confessorship and martyrdom here, who was it that saluted the fair Saxon youths as they passed by him in the streets of the great City, with the salutation, *Salvete flores martyrum*? And when the time came for each in turn to leave that peaceful home, and to go forth to the conflict, to whom did they betake themselves before leaving Rome, to receive a blessing which might nerve them for their work? They went for a saint's blessing; they went to a calm old man, who had never seen blood, except in penance; who had longed indeed to die for Christ, what time the great St Francis opened the way to the far east, but who had been fixed as if a sentinel in the holy city, and walked up and down for fifty years on one beat, while his brethren were in the battle. O the fire of that heart, too great for its frail tenement, which tormented him to be kept at home when the whole Church was at war! And therefore came those bright-haired strangers to him, ere they set out for the scene of their passion, that the full zeal and love pent up in that burning breast might find a vent, and flow over, from him who was kept at home, upon those who were to face the foe. Therefore one by one, each in his turn, those youthful soldiers came to the old man; and one by one they persevered and gained the crown and the palm, all but one, who had not gone, and would not go, for the salutary blessing.

My Fathers, my Brothers, that old man was my own St Philip. Bear with me for his sake. If I have spoken too seriously, his sweet smile shall temper it. As he was with you three centuries ago in Rome, when our Temple fell, so now surely when it is rising, it is a pleasant token that he should have even set out on his travels to you; and that, as if remembering how he interceded for you at home, and recognising the relations he then formed with you, he should now be wishing to have a name among you, and to be loved by you, and perchance to do you a service, here in your own land.

God's Will the End of Life

Reprinted from *Discourses Addressed to Mixed Congregations*

I am going to ask you a question, my dear brethren, so trite, and therefore so uninteresting at first sight, that you may wonder why I put it, and may object that it will be difficult to fix the mind on it, and may anticipate that nothing profitable can be made of it. It is this: "Why were you sent into the world?" Yet, after all, it is perhaps a thought more obvious than it is common, more easy than it is familiar; I mean it ought to come into your minds, but it does not, and you never had more than a distant acquaintance with it, though that sort of acquaintance with it you have had for many years. Nay, once or twice, perhaps you have been thrown across the thought somewhat intimately, for a short season, but this was an accident which did not last. There are those who recollect the first time, as it would seem, when it came home to them. They were but little children, and they were by themselves, and they spontaneously asked themselves, or rather God spake in them, "Why am I here? How came I here? Who brought me here? What am I to do here?"

Perhaps it was the first act of reason, the beginning of their real responsibility, the commencement of their trial; perhaps from that day they may date their capacity, their awful power, of choosing between good and evil, and of committing mortal sin. And so, as life goes on the thought comes vividly, from time to time, for a short season across their conscience; whether in illness, or in some anxiety, or at some season of solitude, or on hearing some preacher, or reading some religious work. A vivid feeling comes over them of the vanity and unprofitableness of the world, and then the question recurs, "Why then am I sent into it?"

And a great contrast indeed does this vain, unprofitable, yet overbearing world present with such a question as that. It seems out of place to ask such a question in so magnificent, so imposing a presence, as that of the great Babylon. The world professes to supply all that we need, as if we were sent into it for the sake of being sent here, and for nothing beyond the sending. It is a great favour to have an introduction to this august world. This is to be our exposition, forsooth, of the mystery of life. Every man is doing his own will here, seeking his own pleasure, pursuing his own ends, and that is why he was brought into existence. Go abroad into the streets of the populous city, contemplate the continuous outpouring there of human energy, and the countless varieties of human character, and be satisfied. The ways are thronged, carriageway and pavement; multitudes are hurrying to and fro, each on his own errand, or are loitering about from listlessness, or from want of work, or have come forth into the public concourse, to see and to be seen, for amusement or for display, or on the excuse of business. The carriages of the wealthy mingle with the slow wains laden with provisions or merchandise, the productions of art or the demands of luxury. The streets are lined with shops, open and gay, inviting customers, and widen now and then into some spacious square or place, with lofty masses of brickwork or of stone, gleaming in the fitful sunbeam, and surrounded or fronted with what simulates a garden's foliage. Follow them in another direction, and you find the whole groundstead covered with large buildings, planted thickly up and down, the homes of the mechanical arts. The air is filled, below, with a ceaseless, importunate, monotonous din, which penetrates even to your most innermost chamber, and rings in your ears even when you are not conscious of it; and overhead, with a canopy of smoke, shrouding God's day from the realms of obstinate sullen toil. This is the end of man!

Or stay at home, and take up one of those daily prints which are so true a picture of the world; look down the columns of advertisements, and you will see the catalogue of pursuits, projects, aims, anxieties, amusements, indulgences which occupy the mind of man. He plays many parts: here he has goods to sell, there he wants employment; there again he seeks to borrow money, here he offers you houses, great seats or small tenements; he has food for the million, and luxuries for the wealthy, and sovereign medicines for the credulous, and books, new and cheap, for the inquisitive. Pass on to the news of the day, and you will learn what great men are doing at home and abroad: you will read of wars and rumours of wars; of debates in the Legislature; of rising men, and old statesmen going off the scene; of political contests in this city or that county; of the collision of rival interests. You will read of the money market, and the provision market, and the market for metals; of the state of trade, the call for manufactures, news of ships arrived in port, of accidents at sea, of exports and imports, of gains and losses, of frauds and their detection. Go forward, and you arrive at discoveries in art and science, discoveries (so-called) in religion, the court and royalty, the entertainments of the great, places of amusement, strange trials, offences, accidents, escapes, exploits, experiments, contests, ventures. O this curious, restless, clamorous, panting being, which we call life! And is there to be no end to all this? Is there no object in it? It never has an end, it is forsooth its own object!

And now, once more my brethren, put aside what you see and what you read of the world, and try to penetrate into the hearts, and to reach the ideas and the feelings of those who constitute it; look into them as closely as you can; enter into their houses and private rooms; strike at random through the streets and lanes: take as they come, palace and hovel, office or factory, and what will you find? Listen to their words, witness, alas! Their works; you will find in the main the same lawless thoughts, the same unrestrained desires, the same ungoverned passions, the same earthly opinions, the same wilful deeds, in high and low, learned and unlearned; you will find them all to be living for the sake of living; they one and all seem to tell you, "We are our own centre, our own end." Why are they toiling? Why are they scheming? For what are they living? "We live to please ourselves; life is worthless except we have our own way; we are not sent here at all, but we find ourselves here, and we are but slaves unless we can think what we will, believe what we will, love what we will, hate what we will, do what we will. We detest interference on the part of God or man. We do not bargain to be rich or to be great; but we do bargain, whether rich or poor, high or low, to live for ourselves, to live for the lust of the moment, or, according to the doctrine of the hour, thinking of the future and the unseen just as much or as little as we please."

O my brethren, is it not a shocking thought, but who can deny its truth? The multitude of men are living without any aim beyond this visible scene; they may from time to time use religious words, or they may profess a communion or a worship, as a matter of course, or of expedience, or of duty, but, if there was any sincerity in such profession, the course of the world could not run as it does. What a contrast is all this to the end of life, as it is set before us in our most holy faith! If there was one amongst the sons of men, who might allowably have taken his pleasure and have done his own will here below, surely it was he who came down on earth from the bosom of the Father, and who was so pure and spotless in that human nature which he put on him, that he could have no human purpose or aim inconsistent with the will of his Father.

Yet he, the Son of God, the Eternal Word, came, not to do his own will, but his who sent him, as you know very well is told us again and again in the Scripture. Thus the Prophet in the Psalter, speaking in his person, says, "Lo, I come to do thy will, O God." And he says in the Prophet Isaias, "The Lord God hath opened mine ear, and I do not resist; I have not gone back." And in the Gospel, when he had come on earth, "My food is to do the will of him that sent me, and to finish his work." Hence, too, in his agony, he cried out, "Not my will, but thine be done;" and St Paul, in like manner, says, that "Christ pleased not himself;" and elsewhere, that, "though he was God's Son, yet learned he obedience by the things which he suffered." Surely so it was; as being indeed the Eternal Co-equal Son, his will was one and the same with the Father's will, and he had no submission of will to make; but he chose to take on him man's nature, and the will of that nature; he chose to take on him affections, feelings, and inclinations proper to man, a will innocent indeed and good, but still a man's will, distinct from God's will; a will, which, had it acted simply according to what was pleasing to its nature, would, when pain and toil were to be endured, have held back from an active co-operation with the will of God. But, though he took on himself the nature of man, he took not on him that selfishness with which fallen man wraps himself round, but in all things he devoted himself as a ready sacrifice to his Father. He came on earth, not to take his pleasure, not to follow his taste, not for the mere exercise of human affection, but simply to glorify his

Father and to do his will. He came charged with a mission, deputed for a work; he looked not to the right nor to the left, he thought not of himself, he offered himself up to God.

Hence it is that he was carried in the womb of a poor woman, who, before his birth, had two journeys to make, of love and of obedience, to the mountains and to Bethlehem. He was born in a stable, and laid in a manger. He was hurried off to Egypt to sojourn there; then he lived till he was thirty years of age in a poor way, by a rough trade, in a small house, in a despised town. Then, when he went out to preach, he had not where to lay his head; he wandered up and down the country, as a stranger upon earth. He was driven out into the wilderness, and dwelt among the wild beasts. He endured heat and cold, hunger and weariness, reproach and calumny. His food was coarse bread, and fish from the lake, or depended on the hospitality of strangers. And as he had already left his Father's greatness on high, and had chosen an earthly home; so again, at that Father's bidding, he gave up the sole solace given him in this world, and denied himself his mother's presence. He parted with her who bore him; he endured to be strange to her: he endured to call her coldly "woman," who was his own undefiled one, all beautiful, all gracious, the best creature of his hands, and the sweet nurse of his infancy. He put her aside, as Levi, his type, merited the sacred ministry, by saying to his parents and kinsmen, "I know you not." He exemplified in his own person the severe maxim which he gave to his disciples, "He that loveth mother more than me is not worthy of me." In all these many ways he sacrificed every wish of his own; that we might understand that, if he, the Creator, came into his own world, not for his own pleasure, but to do his Father's will, we too have most surely some work to do, and have seriously to bethink ourselves what that work is.

Yes, so it is; realise it, my brethren; everyone who breathes, high and low, educated and ignorant, young and old, man and woman, has a mission, has a work. We are not sent into this world for nothing; we are not born at random; we are not here that we may go to bed at night, and get up in the morning, toil for our bread, eat and drink, laugh and joke, sin when we have a mind, and reform when we are tired of sinning, rear a family and die. God sees every one of us; he creates every soul, he lodges it in the body, one by one, for a purpose. He needs, he deigns to need, every one of us. He has an end for each of us; we are all equal in his sight, and we are placed in our different ranks and stations, not to get what we can out of them for ourselves, but to labour in them for him. As Christ has his work, we too have ours; as he rejoiced to do his work, we must rejoice in ours also.

St Paul on one occasion speaks of the world as a scene in a theatre. Consider what is meant by this. You know, actors on a stage are on an equality with each other really, but for the occasion they assume a difference of character; some are high, some are low, some are merry, and some sad. Well, would it not be a simple absurdity in any actor to pride himself on his mock diadem, or his edgeless sword, instead of attending to his part? What, if he did but gaze at himself and his dress? What, if he secreted, or turned to his own use, what was valuable in it? Is it not his business, and nothing else, to act his part well? Common sense tells us so. Now we are all but actors in this world; we are one and all equal, we shall be judged as equals as soon as life is over; yet, equal and similar in ourselves, each has his special part at present, each has his work, each has his mission, not to indulge his passions, not to make money, not to get a name in the world, not to save himself trouble, not to follow his bent, not to be selfish and self-willed, but to do what God puts on him to do.

Look at that poor profligate in the Gospel, look at Dives; do you think he understood that his wealth was to be spent, not on himself, but for the glory of God? Yet for forgetting this, he was lost forever and ever. I will tell you what he thought, and how he viewed things: he was a young man, and had succeeded to a good estate, and he determined to enjoy himself. It did not strike him that his wealth had any other use than that of enabling him to take his pleasure. Lazarus lay at his gate; he might have relieved Lazarus; *that* was God's will; but he managed to put conscience aside, and he persuaded himself he should be a fool, if he did not make the most of this world, while he had the means. So he resolved to have his fill of pleasure; and feasting was to his mind a principal part of it. "He fared sumptuously every day;" everything belonging to him was in the best style, as men speak; his house, his furniture, his plate of silver and gold, his attendants, his establishments. Everything was for enjoyment, and for show too; to attract the eyes of the world, and to gain the applause and admiration of his equals, who were the companions of his sins. These companions were doubtless such as became a person of such pretensions; they were fashionable men; a collection of refined, high-bred, haughty men, eating, not gluttonously, but what was rare and costly; delicate, exact, fastidious in their taste, from their very habits of indulgence; not eating for the mere sake of eating, or drinking for the mere sake of drinking, but making a sort of science of their sensuality; sensual, carnal, as flesh and blood can be, with eyes, ears, tongue, steeped in impurity, every thought, look, and sense, witnessing or ministering to the evil one who ruled them; yet, with exquisite correctness of idea and judgement, laying down rules for sinning; heartless and selfish, high, punctilious, and disdainful in their outward deportment, and shrinking from Lazarus, who lay at the gate, as an eyesore, who ought for the sake of decency to be put out of the way. Dives was one of such, and so he lived his short span, thinking of nothing, loving nothing, but himself, till one day he got into a fatal quarrel with one of his godless associates, or he caught some bad illness; and then he lay helpless on his bed of pain, cursing fortune and his physician, that he was no better, and impatient that he was thus kept from enjoying his youth, trying to fancy himself mending when he was getting worse, and disgusted at those who would not throw him some word of comfort in his suspense, and turning more resolutely from his Creator in proportion to his suffering; and then at last his day came, and he died, and (oh! Miserable!) "was buried in hell." And so ended he and his mission.

This was the fate of your pattern and idol, O ye, if any of you be present, young men, who, though not possessed of wealth and rank, yet affect the fashions of those who have them. You, my brethren, have not been born splendidly or nobly; you have not been brought up in the seats of liberal education; you have no high connections; you have not learned the manners nor caught the tone of good society; you have no share of the largeness of mind, the candour, the romantic sense of honour, the correctness of taste, the consideration for others, and the gentleness which the world puts forth as its highest type of excellence; you have not come near the courts or the mansions of the great; yet you ape the sin of Dives, while you are strangers to his refinement. You think it the sign of a gentleman to set yourselves above religion, to criticise the religious and professors of religion, to look at Catholic and Methodist with impartial contempt, to gain a smattering of knowledge on a number of subjects, to dip into a number of frivolous publications, if they are popular, to have read the latest novel, to have heard the singer and seen the actor of the day, to be well up with the news, to know the names and, if so be, the persons of public men, to be able to bow to them, to walk up and down the street with your heads on high, and to stare at whatever meets you; and to say and do worse things, of which these outward extravagances are but the symbol. And this is what you conceive you have come upon earth for! The Creator made you, it seems, O my children, for this work and office, to be a bad imitation of polished ungodliness, to be a piece of tawdry and faded finery, or a scent which has lost its freshness, and does but offend the sense! O that you could see how absurd and base are such pretences in the eyes of any but yourselves! No calling of life but is honourable; no one is ridiculous who acts suitably to his calling and estate; no one, who has good sense and humility, but may, in any station of life, be truly well-bred and refined; but ostentation, affectation, and ambitious efforts are, in every station of life, high or low, nothing but vulgarities. Put them aside, despise them yourselves, O my very dear sons, whom I love and whom I would fain serve; O that you could feel that you have souls! O that you would have mercy on your souls! O that, before it is too late, you would betake yourselves to him who is the source of all that is truly high and magnificent and beautiful, all that is bright and pleasant, and secure what you ignorantly seek, in him whom you so wilfully, so awfully despise!

He alone, the Son of God, "the brightness of the Eternal Light, and the spotless mirror of his majesty," is the source of all good and all happiness to rich and poor, high and low. If you were ever so high, you would need him; if you were ever so low, you could offend him. The poor can offend him; the poor man can neglect his divinely appointed mission as well as the rich. Do not suppose, my brethren, that what I have said against the upper or the middle class, will not, if you happen to be poor also lie against you. Though a man were as poor as Lazarus, he could be as guilty as Dives. If you are resolved to degrade yourselves to the brutes of the field, who have no reason and no conscience, you need not wealth or rank to enable you to do so. Brutes have no wealth; they have no pride of life; they have no purple and fine linen, no splendid table, no retinue of servants, and yet they are brutes. They are brutes by the law of their nature: they are the poorest among the poor; there is not a vagrant and outcast who is so poor as they; they differ from him, not in their possessions, but in their want of a soul, in that he has a mission and they have not, he can sin and they cannot. O my brethren, it stands to reason, a man may intoxicate himself with a cheap draught, as well as with a costly one; he may steal another's money for his appetites, though he does not waste his own upon them; he may break through the natural and social laws which encircle him, and profane the sanctity of family duties, though he be, not a child of nobles, but a peasant or artisan, nay, and perhaps he does so more frequently than they. This is not the poor's blessedness, that he has less temptations to self-indulgence, for he has as many, but that from his circumstances he receives the penances and corrections of self-indulgence. Poverty is the mother of many pains and sorrows in their season, and these are God's messengers to lead the soul to repentance; but, alas! If the poor man indulges his passions, thinks little of religion, puts off repentance, refuses to make an effort, and dies without conversion, it matters nothing that he was poor in this world, it matters nothing that he was less daring than the rich, it matters not that he promised himself God's favour, that he sent for the priest when death came, and received the last Sacraments; Lazarus too, in that case, shall be buried with Dives in hell, and shall have had his consolation neither in this world nor in the world to come.

My brethren, the simple question is, whatever a man's rank in life may be, does he in that rank perform the work which God has given him to do? Now then, let me turn to others, of a very different description, and let me hear what they will say, when the question is asked them; why, they will parry it thus: "You give us no alternative," they will say to me, "except that of being sinners or saints. You put before us Our Lord's pattern, and you spread before us the guilt and the ruin of the deliberate transgressor; whereas we have no intention of going so far one way or the other; we do not aim at being saints, but we have no desire at all to be sinners. We neither intend to disobey God's will, nor to give up our own. Surely there is a middle way, and a safe one, in which God's will and our will may both be satisfied. We mean to enjoy both this world and the next. We will guard against mortal sin; we are not obliged to guard against venial; indeed it would be endless to attempt it. None but saints do so; it is the work of a life; we need have nothing else to do. We are not monks, we are in the world, we are in business, we are parents, we have families; we must live for the day. It is a consolation to keep from mortal sin; that we do, and it is enough for salvation. It is a great thing to keep in God's favour; what indeed can we desire more?

We come at due time to the sacraments; this is our comfort and our stay; did we die, we should die in grace, and escape the doom of the wicked. But if we once attempted to go further, where should we stop? How will you draw the line for us? The line between mortal and venial sin is very distinct; we understand that; but do you not see that, if we attended to our venial sins, there would be just as much reason to attend to one as to another? If we began to repress our anger, why not also repress vainglory? Why not also guard against niggardliness? Why not also keep from falsehood, from gossiping, from idling, from excess in eating? And, after all, without venial sin we never can be, unless indeed we have the prerogative of the Mother of God, which it would be almost heresy to ascribe to anyone but her. You are not asking us to be converted; that we understand; we *are* converted, we were converted a long time ago. You bid us aim at an indefinite vague something, which is less than perfection, yet more than obedience, and which, without resulting in any tangible advantage, debars us from the pleasures and embarrasses us in the duties of this world."

This is what you will say; but your premises, my brethren, are better than your reasoning, and your conclusions will not stand. You have a right view why God has sent you into the world, viz., in order that you may get to heaven; it is quite true also that you would fare well indeed if you found yourselves there, you could desire nothing better; nor, it is true, can any live any time without venial sin. It is true also that you are not obliged to aim at being saints; it is no sin not to aim at perfection. So much is true and to the purpose; but it does not follow from it that you, with such views and feelings as you have expressed, are using sufficient exertions even for attaining to purgatory. Has your religion any difficulty in it, or is it in all respects easy to you? Are you simply taking your own pleasure in your mode of living, or do you find your pleasure in submitting yourself to God's pleasure? In a word, is your religion a work? For if it be not, it is not religion at all. Here at once, before going into your argument, is a proof that it is an unsound one, because it brings you to the conclusion that, whereas Christ came to do a work, and all saints, nay, nay, and sinners do a work too, you, on the contrary, have no work to do, because, forsooth, you are neither sinners nor saints; or, if you once had a work, at least that you have despatched it already, and you have nothing upon your hands. You have attained your salvation, it seems, before your time, and have nothing to occupy you, and are detained on earth too long. The work days are over, and your perpetual holiday is begun. Did then God send you, above all other men, into the world to be idle in spiritual matters? Is it your mission only to find pleasure in this world, in which you are but as pilgrims and sojourners? Are you more than sons of Adam, who, by the sweat of their brow, are to eat bread till they return to the earth out of which they are taken? Unless you have some work in hand, unless you are struggling, unless you are fighting with yourselves, you are no followers of those who "through

many tribulations entered into the kingdom of God."
A fight is the very token of a Christian. He is a soldier
of Christ; high or low, he is this and nothing else. If
you have triumphed over all mortal sin, as you seem to
think, then you must attack your venial sins; there is no
help for it; there is nothing else to do, if you would be
soldiers of Jesus Christ. But, O simple souls! To think
you have gained any triumph at all! No: you cannot
safely be at peace with any, even the least malignant, of
the foes of God; if you are at peace with venial sins, be
certain that in their company and under their shadow
mortal sins are lurking. Mortal sins are the children of
venial, which, though they be not deadly themselves,
yet are prolific of death. You may think that you have
killed the giants who had possession of your hearts,
and that you have nothing to fear, but may sit at rest
under your vine and under your fig-tree; but the giants
will live again, they will rise from the dust, and, before
you know where you are, you will be taken captive
and slaughtered by the fierce, powerful, and eternal
enemies of God.

The end of a thing is the test. It was Our Lord's
rejoicing in his last solemn hours, that he had done
the work for which he was sent. "I have glorified thee
on earth," he says in his prayer, "I have finished the
work which thou gavest me to do; I have manifested
thy name to the men whom thou hast given me out
of the world." It was St Paul's consolation also; "I
have fought the good fight, I have finished the course,
I have kept the faith; henceforth there is laid up for
me a crown of justice, which the Lord shall render to

me in that day, the just Judge." Alas! alas! How different will be our view of things when we come to die, or when we have passed into eternity, from the dreams and pretences with which we beguile ourselves now! What will Babel do for us then? Will it rescue our souls from the purgatory or the hell to which it sends them? If we were created, it was that we might serve God; if we have his gifts, it is that we may glorify him; if we have a conscience, it is that we may obey it; if we have the prospect of heaven, it is that we may keep it before us; if we have light, that we might follow it; if we have grace, that we may save ourselves by means of it. Alas! Alas! For those who die without fulfilling their mission! Who were called to be holy, and lived in sin; Who were called to worship Christ, and who plunged into this giddy and unbelieving world; who were called to fight, and who remained idle; who were called to be Catholics, and who did but remain in the religion of their birth! Alas for those who have had gifts and talent, and have not used, or have misused, or abused them; who have had wealth, and have spent it on themselves; who have had abilities, and have advocated what was sinful, or ridiculed what was true, or scattered doubts against what was sacred; who have had leisure, and have wasted it on wicked companions, or evil books, or foolish amusements! Alas for those of whom the best that can be said is that they are harmless and naturally blameless, while they never have attempted to cleanse their hearts or to live in God's sight!

The world goes on from age to age, but the holy angels and blessed saints are always crying, "Alas, alas!"

and "Woe, woe!" over the loss of vocations, and the disappointment of hopes, and the scorn of God's love, and the ruin of souls. One generation succeeds another, and whenever they look down upon earth from their golden thrones, they see scarcely anything but a multitude of guardian spirits, downcast and sad, each following his own charge, in anxiety, or in terror, or in despair, vainly endeavouring to shield him from the enemy, and failing because he will not be shielded. Times come and go, and man will not believe, that that is to be which is not yet, or that what now is only continues for a season, and is not eternity. The end is the trial; the world passes; it is but a pageant and a scene; the lofty palace crumbles, the busy city is mute, the ships of Tarshish have sped away. On heart and flesh death is coming; the veil is breaking. Departing soul, how hast thou used thy talents, thy opportunities, the light poured around thee, the warning given thee, the grace inspired into thee? O my Lord and Saviour, support me in that hour in the strong arms of thy sacraments, and by the fresh fragrance of thy consolations. Let the absolving words be said over me, and the holy oil sign and seal me, and thy own Body be my food, and thy Blood my sprinkling; and let my sweet mother Mary breathe on me, and my angel whisper peace to me, and my glorious saints, and my own dear father, Philip, smile on me; that in them all, and through them all, I may receive the gift of perseverance, and die, as I desire to live, in thy faith, in thy Church, in thy service, and in thy love.

The Assumption of the
Blessed Virgin Mary

First published in *Discourses Addressed to Mixed Congregations*,
under the title "The Fitness of the Glories of Mary".

You may recollect, my brethren, Our Lord's words
when on the day of his resurrection he had joined
the two disciples on their way to Emmaus, and found
them sad and perplexed in consequence of his death.
He said, "Ought not Christ to suffer these things, and
so enter into his glory?" He appealed to the fitness
and congruity which existed between this otherwise
surprising event and the other truths which had been
revealed concerning the divine purpose of saving
the world. And so, too, St Paul, in speaking of the
same wonderful appointment of God; "It became
him," he says, "for whom are all things, and through
whom are all things, who had brought many sons unto
glory, to consummate the author of their salvation by
suffering." Elsewhere, speaking of prophesying, or the
exposition of what is latent in divine truth, he bids his
brethren exercise the gift, "according to the analogy
or rule of faith"; that is, so that the doctrine preached
may correspond and fit into what is already received.

Thus, you see, it is a great evidence of truth, in the case of revealed teaching, that it is so consistent, that it so hangs together, that one thing springs out of another, that each part requires and is required by the rest.

This great principle, which is exemplified so variously in the structure and history of Catholic doctrine, which will receive more and more illustrations the more carefully and minutely we examine the subject, is brought before us especially at this season, when we are celebrating the Assumption of our Blessed Lady, the Mother of God, into heaven. We receive it on the belief of ages; but, viewed in the light of reason, it is the fitness of this termination of her earthly course which so persuasively recommends it to our minds: we feel it "ought" to be; that it "becomes" her Lord and Son thus to provide for one who was so singular and special, both in herself and her relations to him. We find that it is simply in harmony with the substance and main outlines of the doctrine of the Incarnation, and that without it Catholic teaching would have a character of incompleteness, and would disappoint our pious expectations.

Let us direct our thoughts to this subject today, my brethren; and with a view of helping you to do so, I will first state what the Church has taught and defined from the first ages concerning the Blessed Virgin, and then you will see how naturally the devotion which her children show her, and the praises with which they honour her, follow from it.

Now, as you know, it has been held from the first, and defined from an early age, that Mary is the Mother of God. She is not merely the Mother of Our Lord's manhood, or of Our Lord's body, but she is to be considered the mother of the Word himself, the Word incarnate. God, in the person of the Word, the Second Person of the All-glorious Trinity, humbled himself to become her Son. *Non horruisti Virginis uterum,* as the Church sings, "Thou didst not disdain the Virgin's womb." He took the substance of his human flesh from her, and clothed in it he lay within her; and he bore it about with him after birth, as a sort of badge and witness that he, though God, was hers. He was nursed and tended by her; he was suckled by her; he lay in her arms. As time went on, he ministered to her, and obeyed her. He lived with her for thirty years, in one house, with an uninterrupted intercourse, and with only the saintly Joseph to share it with him. She was the witness of his growth, of his joys, of his sorrows, of his prayers; she was blest with his smile, with the touch of his hand, with the whisper of his affection, with the expression of his thoughts and his feelings, for that length of time. Now, my brethren, what ought she to be, what is it becoming that she should be, who was so favoured?

Such a question was once asked by a heathen king, when he would place one of his subjects in a dignity becoming the relation in which the latter stood towards him. That subject had saved the king's life, and what was to be done to him in return? The king asked, "What should be done to the man whom the king desireth to honour?" And he received the following answer: "The man whom the king wisheth to honour ought to be clad in the king's apparel, and to be mounted on the king's saddle, and to receive the royal diadem on his head; and let the first among the king's princes and presidents hold his horse, and let him walk through the streets of the city, and say, 'Thus shall he be honoured, whom the king hath a mind to honour.'" So stands the case with Mary; she gave birth to the Creator, and what recompense shall be made her? What shall be done to her, who had this relationship to the Most High? What shall be the fit accompaniment of one whom the Almighty has deigned to make, not his servant, not his friend, not his intimate, but his superior, the source of his second being, the nurse of his helpless infancy, the teacher of his opening years? I answer, as the king was answered: Nothing is too high for her to whom God owes his human life; no exuberance of grace, no excess of glory, but is becoming, but is to be expected there, where God has lodged himself, whence God has issued. Let her "be clad in the king's apparel," that is, let the fullness of the Godhead so flow into her that she may be a figure of the incommunicable sanctity, and beauty, and glory, of God himself: that she may be the Mirror of Justice, the Mystical Rose, the Tower of Ivory, the House of Gold, the Morning Star. Let her "receive the king's diadem upon her head," as the Queen of heaven, the Mother of all living, the Health of the Weak, the Refuge of Sinners, the Comforter of the Afflicted. And "let the first amongst the king's princes walk before her," let angels and prophets, and apostles, and martyrs, and all saints, kiss the hem of her garment and rejoice under the shadow of her throne.

Thus is it that King Solomon has risen up to meet his mother, and bowed himself unto her, and caused a seat to be set for the king's mother, and she sits on his right hand.

We should be prepared, then, my brethren, to believe that the Mother of God is full of grace and glory, from the very fitness of such a dispensation, even though we had not been taught it; and this fitness will appear still more clear and certain when we contemplate the subject more steadily. Consider, then, that it has been the ordinary rule of God's dealings with us, that personal sanctity should be the attendant upon high spiritual dignity of place or work. The angels, who, as the word imports, are God's messengers, are also perfect in holiness; "without sanctity, no one shall see God": no defiled thing can enter the courts of heaven; and the higher its inhabitants are advanced in their ministry: about the throne, the holier are they, and the more absorbed in their contemplation of that Holiness upon which they wait. The Seraphim, who immediately surround the Divine Glory, cry day and night, "Holy, Holy, Holy, Lord God of Hosts"! So is it also on earth; the prophets have ordinarily not only gifts but graces; they are not only inspired to know and to teach God's will, but inwardly converted to obey it. For surely those only can preach the truth duly who feel it personally; those only transmit it fully from God to man, who have in the transmission made it their own.

I do not say that there are no exceptions to this rule, but they admit of an easy explanation; I do not say that it never pleases Almighty God to convey an intimation of his will through bad men; of course, for all things can be made to serve him. By all, even the wicked, he accomplishes his purposes, and by the wicked he is glorified. Our Lord's death was brought about by his enemies, who did his will, while they thought they were gratifying their own. Caiaphas, who contrived and effected it, was made use of to predict it. Balaam prophesied good of God's people in an earlier age, by a divine compulsion, when he wished to prophesy evil. This is true; but in such cases Divine Mercy is plainly overruling the evil, and manifesting his power, without recognising or sanctioning the instrument. And again, it is true, as he tells us himself, that in the last day "Many shall say, Lord, Lord, have we not prophesied in thy name, and in thy name cast out devils, and done many miracles?" And that he shall answer, "I never knew you." This, I say, is undeniable; it is undeniable first, that those who have prophesied in God's name may afterwards fall from God, and lose their souls. Let a man be ever so holy now, he may fall away; and, as present grace is no pledge of perseverance, much less are present gifts; but how does this show that gifts and graces do not commonly go together? Again, it is undeniable that those who have had miraculous gifts may nevertheless have never been in God's favour, not even when they exercised them; as I will explain presently. But I am now speaking, not of having gifts, but of being prophets. To be a prophet is something much more personal than to possess gifts. It is a sacred office, it implies a mission, and is the high distinction, not of the enemies of God, but of his friends. Such is the Scripture rule. Who was the first prophet and preacher of justice? Enoch, who walked "by faith," and "pleased God," and was taken from a rebellious world. Who was the second? "Noah," who "condemned the world, and was made heir of the justice which is through faith." Who was the next great prophet? Moses, the lawgiver of the chosen people, who was the "meekest of all men who dwell on the earth." Samuel comes next, who served the Lord from his infancy in the Temple; and then David, who, if he fell into sin, repented, and was "a man after God's heart." And in like manner Job, Elias, Isaias, Jeremias, Daniel, and above them all St John the Baptist, and then again St Peter, St Paul, St John, and the rest, are all especial instances of heroic virtue, and patterns to their brethren. Judas is the exception, but this was by a particular dispensation to enhance Our Lord's humiliation and suffering.

Nature itself witnesses to this connection between sanctity and truth. It anticipates that the fountain from which pure doctrine comes should itself be pure; that the seat of divine teaching, and the oracle of faith should be the abode of angels; that the consecrated home, in which the word of God is elaborated, and whence it issues forth for the salvation of the many, should be holy, as that word itself is holy. Here you see the difference of the office of a prophet and a mere gift, such as that of miracles. Miracles are the simple and direct work of God; the worker of them is but an instrument or organ. And in consequence he need not be holy, because he has not, strictly speaking, a share in the work. So again the power of administering the sacraments, which also is supernatural and miraculous, does not imply personal holiness; nor is there anything surprising in God's giving to a bad man this gift, or the gift of miracles, any more than in his giving him any natural talent or gift, strength or agility of frame, eloquence, or medical skill. It is otherwise with the office of preaching and prophesying, and to this I have been referring; for the truth first goes into the minds of the speakers, and is apprehended and fashioned there, and then comes out from them as, in one sense, its source and its parent. The Divine Word is begotten in them, and the offspring has their features and tells of them. They are not like "the dumb animal, speaking with man's voice," on which Balaam rode, a mere instrument of God's word, but they have "received an unction from the Holy One, and they know all things"' and "where the Spirit of the Lord is, there is liberty": and while they deliver what they have received, they enforce what they feel and know. "We have known and believed," says St John, "the charity which God hath to us."

So has it been all through the history of the Church: Moses does not write as David; nor Isaias as Jeremias: nor St John as St Paul. And so of the great doctors of the Church, St Athanasius, St Augustine, St Ambrose, St Leo, St Thomas, each has his own manner, each speaks his own words, though he speaks the while the words of God. They speak from themselves, they speak in their own persons, they speak from the heart, from their own experience, with their own arguments, with their own deductions, with their own modes of expression. Now can you fancy, my brethren, such hearts, such feelings to be unholy? How could it be so, without defiling, and thereby nullifying, the word of God? If one drop of corruption makes the purest water worthless, as the slightest savour of bitterness spoils the most delicate viands, how can it be that the word of truth and holiness can proceed profitably from impure lips and an earthly heart? No; as is the tree, so is the fruit. "Beware of false prophets," says Our Lord, and then he adds, "From their fruits ye shall know them. Do men gather grapes of thorns, or figs of thistles?" Is it not so, my brethren? Which of you would go to ask counsel of another, however learned, however gifted, however aged, if you thought him unholy? Nay, though you feel and are sure, as far as absolution goes, that a bad priest could give it as really as a holy priest, yet for advice, for comfort, for instruction, you would not go to one whom you did not respect. "Out of the abundance of the heart, the mouth speaketh"; "a good man out of the good treasure of his heart bringeth forth good, and an evil man out of the evil treasure bringeth forth evil."

So, then, is it in the case of the soul; but, as regards the Blessed Mary, a further thought suggests itself. She has no chance place in the divine dispensation; the Word of God did not merely come to her and go from her; he did not pass through her, as he visits us in Holy Communion. It was no heavenly body which the Eternal Son assumed, fashioned by the angels, and brought down to this lower world: no; he imbibed, he absorbed into his divine Person her blood and the substance of her flesh, by becoming man of her. He received her lineaments and features, as the appropriate character in which he was to manifest himself to mankind. The child is like the parent, and we may well suppose that by his likeness to her was manifested her relationship to him. Her sanctity comes, not only of her being his mother, but also of his being her son. "If the first fruit be holy," says St Paul, "the mass also is holy; if the mass be holy, so are the branches." And hence the titles which we are accustomed to give her. He is the Wisdom of God, she therefore is the Seat of Wisdom; his presence is heaven, she therefore is the Gate of Heaven; he is infinite mercy, she then is the Mother of Mercy. She is the mother of "fair love and fear, and knowledge and holy hope"; is it wonderful, then, that she has left behind her in the Church below "an odour like cinnamon and balm, and sweetness like to choice myrrh"?

Such, then, is the truth ever cherished in the deep heart of the Church, and witnessed by the keen apprehension of her children, that no limits but those proper to a creature can be assigned to the sanctity of Mary. Therefore, did Abraham believe that a son should be born to him of his aged wife? Then Mary's faith must be held as greater when she accepted Gabriel's message. Did Judith consecrate her widowhood to God to the surprise of her people? Much more did Mary, from her first youth, devote her virginity. Did Samuel, when a child, inhabit the Temple, secluded from the world? Mary too was by her parents lodged in the same holy precincts, even at the age when children first can choose between good and evil. Was Solomon on his birth called "dear to the Lord"? And shall not the destined Mother of God be dear to him from the moment she was born? But further still; St John the Baptist was sanctified by the Spirit before his birth; shall Mary be only equal to him? Is it not fitting that her privilege should surpass his? Is it wonderful, if grace, which anticipated his birth by three months, should in her case run up to the very first moment of her being, outstrip the imputation of sin, and be beforehand with the usurpation of Satan? Mary must surpass all the saints; the very fact that certain privileges are known to have been theirs persuades us, almost from the necessity of the case, that she had the same and higher. Her conception was immaculate, in order that she might surpass all saints in the date as well as the fullness of her sanctification.

But in a festive season, my dear brethren, I must not weary you with argument, when we should offer specially to the Blessed Virgin the homage of our love and loyalty; yet, let me finish as I have begun: I will be brief, but bear with me if I view her bright Assumption, as I have viewed her immaculate purity, rather as a point of doctrine than as a theme for devotion.

It was surely fitting, then, it was becoming, that she should be taken up into heaven and not lie in the grave till Christ's second coming, who had passed a life of sanctity and of miracle such as hers. All the works of God are in a beautiful harmony; they are carried on to the end as they begin. This is the difficulty which men of the world find in believing miracles at all; they think these break the order and consistency of God's visible word, not knowing that they do but subserve a higher order of things, and introduce a supernatural perfection. But at least, my brethren, when one miracle is wrought, it may be expected to draw others after it for the completion of what is begun. Miracles must be wrought for some great end; and if the course of things fell back again into a natural order before its termination, how could we but feel a disappointment? And if we were told that this certainly was to be, how could we but judge the information improbable and difficult to believe?

Now this applies to the history of Our Lady. I say, it would be a greater miracle if, her life being what it was, her death was like that of other men, than if it were such as to correspond to her life. Who can conceive, my brethren, that God should so repay the debt, which he condescended to owe to his Mother, for the elements of his human body, as to allow the flesh and blood from which it was taken to moulder in the grave? Do the sons of men thus deal with their mothers? Do they not nourish and sustain them in their feebleness, and keep them in life while they are able? Or who can conceive that that virginal frame, which never sinned, was to undergo the death of a sinner? Why should she share the curse of Adam, who had no share in his fall? "Dust thou art, and into dust thou shalt return," was the sentence upon sin; she, then, who was not a sinner, fitly never saw corruption. She died, then, as we hold because even Our Lord and Saviour died; she died, as she suffered, because she was in this world, because she was in a state of things in which suffering and death are the rule. She lived under their external sway; and as he obeyed Caesar by coming for enrolment to Bethlehem, so did she, when God willed it, yield to the tyranny of death, and was dissolved into soul and body, as well as others. But though she died as well as others, she died not as others die; for, through the merits of her Son, by whom she was what she was, by the grace of Christ which in her had anticipated sin, which had filled her with light, which had purified her flesh from all defilement, she was also saved from disease and malady, and all that weakens and decays the bodily frame. Original sin had not been found in her, by the wear of her senses, and the waste of her frame and the decrepitude of years, propagating death. She died, but her death was a mere fact, not an effect; and, when it was over, it ceased to be. She died that she might live, she died as a matter of form or (as I may call it) an observance, in order to fulfil what is called the debt of nature – not primarily for herself or because of sin, but to submit herself to her condition, to glorify God, to do what her Son did; not, however, as her Son and Saviour, with any suffering for any special end; not with a martyr's death, for her martyrdom had been in living; not as an atonement, for man could not make it, and One had made it, and made it for all; but in order to finish her course, and to receive her crown.

And therefore she died in private. It became him, who died for the world, to die in the world's sight; it became the Great Sacrifice to be lifted up on high, as a light that could not be hid. But she, the lily of Eden, who had always dwelt out of the sight of man, fittingly did she die in the garden's shade, and amid the sweet flowers in which she had lived. Her departure made no noise in the world. The Church went about her common duties, preaching, converting, suffering; there were persecutions, there was fleeing from place to place, there were martyrs, there were triumphs; at length the rumour spread abroad that the Mother of God was no longer upon earth. Pilgrims went to and fro; they sought for her relics, but they found them not; did she die at Ephesus, or did she die at Jerusalem? Reports varied; but her tomb could not be pointed out, or if it was found, it was open; and instead of her pure and fragrant body, there was a growth of lilies from the earth which she had touched. So inquirers went home marvelling, and waiting for further light. And then it was said, how that when her dissolution was at hand, and her soul was to pass in triumph before the judgement-seat of her Son, the apostles were suddenly gathered together in the place, even in the Holy City, to bear part in the joyful ceremonial; how that they buried her with fitting rites; how that the third day, when they came to the tomb, they found it empty, and angelic choirs with their glad voices were heard singing day and night the glories of their risen Queen. But, however we feel towards the details of this history (nor is there anything in it which will be unwelcome or difficult to piety), so much cannot be doubted, from the consent of the whole Catholic world and the revelations made to holy souls, that, as is befitting, she is, soul and body, with her Son and God in heaven, and that we are enabled to celebrate, not only her death, but her Assumption.

And now, my dear brethren, what is befitting in us, if all that I have been telling you is befitting in Mary? If the Mother of Emmanuel ought to be the first of creatures in sanctity and in beauty; if it became her to be free from all sin from the very first, and from the moment she received her first grace to begin to merit more; and if such as was her beginning, such was her end, her conception immaculate and her death an assumption; if she died, but revived, and is exalted on high; what is befitting in the children of such a Mother, but an imitation, in their measure, of her devotion, her meekness, her simplicity, her modesty, and her sweetness? Her glories are not only for the sake of her Son, they are for our sakes also. Let us copy her faith, who received God's message by the angel without a doubt; her patience, who endured St Joseph's surprise without a word; her obedience, who went up to Bethlehem in the winter and bore Our Lord in a stable; her meditative spirit, who pondered in her heart what she saw and heard about him; her fortitude, whose heart the sword went through; her self-surrender, who gave him up during his ministry and consented to his death.

Above all, let us imitate her purity, who, rather than relinquish her virginity, was willing to lose him for a Son. Oh, my dear children, young men and young women, what need have you of the intercession of the Virgin Mother, of her help, of her pattern, in this respect! What shall bring you forward in the narrow way, if you live in the world, but the thought and patronage of Mary? What shall seal your senses, what shall tranquillise your heart, when sights and sounds of danger are around you, but Mary? What shall give you patience and endurance, when you are wearied out with the length of the conflict with evil, with the unceasing necessity of precautions, with the irksomeness of observing them, with the tediousness of their repetition, with the strain upon your mind, with your forlorn and cheerless condition, but a loving communion with her? She will comfort you in your discouragements, solace you in your fatigues, raise you after your falls, reward you for your successes. She will show you her Son, your God and your all. When your spirit within you is excited, or relaxed, or depressed, when it loses its balance, when it is restless and wayward, when it is sick of what it has, and hankers after what it has not, when your eye is solicited with evil and your mortal frame trembles under the shadow of the tempter, what will bring you to yourselves, to peace and to health, but the cool breath of the Immaculate and the fragrance of the Rose of Sharon? It is the boast of the Catholic religion that it has the gift of making the young heart chaste; and why is this, but that it gives us Jesus Christ for our food, and Mary for our nursing Mother? Fulfil this boast in yourselves; prove to the world that you are following no false teaching, vindicate the glory of your Mother Mary, whom the world blasphemes, in the very face of the world, by the simplicity of your own deportment, and the sanctity of your words and deeds. Go to her for the royal heart of innocence. She is the beautiful gift of God, which outshines the fascinations of a bad world, and which no one ever sought in sincerity and was disappointed. She is the personal type and representative image of that spiritual life and renovation in grace, "without which no one shall see God." "Her spirit is sweeter than honey, and her heritage than the honeycomb. They that eat her shall yet be hungry, and they that drink her shall still thirst. Who so hearkeneth to her shall not be confounded, and they that work by her shall not sin."